WINDJAMMERS
of the
MAINE COAST

WINDJAMMERS
of the
MAINE COAST

Written and Illustrated by

Harry W. Smith

Down East Books / Camden, Maine

ISBN: 0-89272-120-0 (hardcover)
       0-89272-135-9 (softcover)
Library of Congress Catalog Card Number: 81-70960
Designed by Harry W. Smith
Typography by Camden Type 'n Graphics, Camden, Maine
Printed in the United States of America

Down East Books
Camden, Maine

Dedicated to the captains and their families,
without whose efforts these vessels would be lost forever.

Contents

Color Plates

Acknowledgments

Although this book covers only one basic type of sailing vessel, the American fore-and aft schooner, the history of the commercial vessels now in Maine covers a period of over a hundred years and many different areas along the Eastern seaboard. Without the assistance of the individual captains, it would have been impossible to compile this work. I would like to give a special thanks to Captain John Foss, Captain Havilah S. Hawkins, Captain W. J. L. Parker, Neil Hotchkiss, and Ms. Dorothy Seits. I also thank my editor, Leon Ballou, for his patience and understanding, and Karin Womer for her assistance. Finally, I thank my wife, Marsha, for her help and inspiration, and my son, Michael, for getting me close enough in his 13-foot whaler, *Pegasus*, to capture the schooners under sail.

Introduction

"All hands ready on the main halyards!" the first mate shouts.

Crew and passengers line up along the deck, taking the large hemp rope in their hands.

Slowly the yawl boat pushes the schooner into the wind. The captain waits until everything is ready, then signals the first mate to raise the mainsail.

"Heave away!" the mate commands.

Hand-over-hand the shipmates pull on the rope, slowly raising the gaff and the huge canvas sail.

"One more tug!" the mate shouts as the sail is pulled taut.

"Now hold the line steady until it is cleated."

When the halyards have been secured around the belaying pins on the ship's rail, the eager crew prepares to raise the smaller foresail and jibs.

When all of the sails are up, the captain eases the helm and the sails fill with wind. The yawl boat is shut down and hurriedly raised on the schooner's stern davits as the vessel begins to build up speed. The fresh breeze pushes against the canvas, forcing the wooden hull through the water. The bow cuts into the blue sea, churning it into foam. Salt spray splashes on the pine decks, making them glisten in the morning sun.

Soon the harbor is far behind, the week-long journey has begun. For many on board this will be their first time at sea; for others, it is a pleasant reunion.

For everyone aboard the wooden sailing schooner it will be a journey into the past, a step back into the maritime history of our nation. There will be no phones, no radios, no television, and in some cases, no electricity or running water for the next six days.

These will be replaced by the sights, the smells, and the sounds of the sea aboard a sailing windjammer, cruising the beautiful coast of Maine. These 20th-century luxuries will not be missed. No one will even mention them as they spend an unforgettable week meeting new friends and shipmates, reading a book in a quiet corner on deck, or watching the seals and dolphins play alongside the schooner. The beauty of the islands, the fragrance of the wild rose, the refrain of the song sparrow will be entertainment beyond compare. Yet, nature is not the only reward; songs sung around the stove in the main cabin, food prepared from scratch on board, lobster and clams baked on the shores of a deserted island are just a few of the experiences that lie ahead. New experiences in an age-old world.

The memories that build as each day progresses will not soon be forgotten. In fact, nearly half the passengers that sail the coast of Maine aboard the windjammer fleet are return passengers.

When I began writing this book I asked each of the captains, "Who sails aboard your vessel and why do they come?" Each time the answer was the same. People of all walks of life, factory workers, doctors, secretaries, college students, and professors come for a week of excitement, memories, and a taste of how our forefathers lived.

Most of the schooners have served in many capacities over the years, but none more interesting than helping people relax and enjoy life.

All of the schooners are Coast Guard inspected and equipped with modern safety devices. Each captain is licensed and the crews are trained to handle any situation. However, these things are not why people decide to spend a week sailing on a vessel some of which are over a century old. The passengers are on board to experience a different and challenging way of life. The windjammers are one of the few ways left to us that allow us to live in the past. Not just walk through a piece of our history, but live it. These sailing schooners are the ultimate working museum. Not everyone expects the same results from this experience. For some it is the slower pace of life, for others the chance to get away from the computer age and use their hands, and for a few it is the thrill and excitement of racing another schooner across the bay under a fresh breeze with salt spray in the air.

The romance of the sea can have lasting effects. Many of today's windjammer captains were first introduced to the sea as passengers aboard the schooners. In some cases the romance went beyond the sea, several captains and crew members have met their wives during a cruise and many passengers have fallen in love while sailing the coast of Maine.

Each Sunday evening brings together a group of strangers from across the country who will sail together, work together, eat together, and explore the wonders of Maine together for a week. On Saturday afternoon they will be friends and crew members. Many of those friendships will last forever. Yet there is plenty of room on board a windjammer to be alone. Their spacious decks have countless places to hide and read a book or contemplate the wonders of nature. The rest of the world and its problems disappear standing at the bow of a schooner watching it cut through the sea, or lying on a cabin top counting the endless stars on a clear summer night. Life aboard the schooners is not structured. There are no cruise directors. Each person sets his own pace, participating in the running of the vessel to the degree he desires. I have sailed on many of the windjammers and have been amazed at how many different activities can be pursued on a vessel. One moonlit evening I rowed from my sloop to a windjammer anchored nearby. At the bow of the schooner a couple sat alone, huddled in a blanket watching the moon rise among the islands. On deck, amidships, several passengers were singing songs led by a crew member with a guitar. Near the helm, the captain was telling stories about sailing and the sea. In the main cabin, a group of passengers were eating brownies and playing charades, while in the galley a few good souls were helping the cook wash the dishes.

Home-cooked meals are a very important part of each cruise. The cook is up at the crack of dawn stoking the old wood stove and brewing a pot of hot coffee. Everything is prepared on board including the bread and pies. Mealtime on a windjammer is a chance for everyone to share their experiences as they eat a delicious meal guaranteed to satisfy the heartiest appetite.

Sailing aboard a Maine windjammer is a total experience, steeped in history, filled with excitement and set in an atmosphere of breathtaking beauty. Rocky cliffs, quiet coves, lighthouses, harbors filled with fishing vessels, lobstermen tending their traps, and other schooners—all of these things are more meaningful from the water. Much of Maine's shoreline lies along a myriad of small peninsulas bounded by private property. The windjammers are the perfect solution to enjoying the true rustic splendor of Maine.

As with any business, there will be changes. The number of schooners will vary over the years as will the names of their owners and captains. Some vessels may leave Maine to sail on other seas and be replaced by new additions to the fleet. A few schooners appear in Maine waters only occasionally, while others are chartered for day sails. My intent in this book is not to account for every schooner on the coast, but rather, to give the reader an insight into the history and romance of these ageless vessels that now sail along Maine's shore.

On the following pages I have illustrated what life aboard a windjammer is all about. I have sketched some of the interesting parts of each vessel, the activities that take place during the week, and studies of nature found as you sail among the islands. For those of you who have sailed on the windjammers, I hope this book will bring back fond memories; for those of you who are about to sail, use it as a guide to what you are about to experience; and to everyone else, I hope it will let you step into the wonderful realm of sailing aboard a fore-and-aft schooner along the coast of Maine.

A Brief History of Fore-and-Aft Schooners

Of all the places in the world, Maine is unique. Her coast was formed by ice age glaciers that sculptured a myriad of channels and inlets protected by thousands of islands. For ages the coast was battered by ice floes carried south on the Labrador current, creating a rough, rockbound texture. Thus, centuries of glaciers, ice floes, and tides shaped a shoreline that measures approximately 220 miles in a straight line into a tidal length of more than 2,500 miles. From sandy beaches to rocky shores, from tidal wetlands to Mount Cadillac, Maine has a coast like no other. Along her shoreline people are born to follow the sea; for more than three centuries they have made their mark shipbuilding and seafaring.

One of the finest examples of how Maine shipbuilders adapted to changing economic conditions is the evolution of the fore-and-aft schooner.

There are two opposing views as to the origin of the fore-and-aft schooner rig. One view is that the rig is an extension of the early sprit sail, which developed around the first century A.D. Over the years as materials such as canvas, rope, and iron work improved, the size of the sails was increased. Eventually, a gaff was added to support the upper edge of the sail, and later a boom along the foot. Rigs of this type were reported in Holland as early as the 17th century. These statements challenged the popular belief held earlier in North America that Captain Robinson of Gloucester invented the schooner in 1713. In all probability, the development of the fore-and-aft rig occurred through several stages in different parts of the world, with local types following their own evolution. Whatever the origin of the schooner, it does not diminish the part the colonial designers played in developing this versatile rig into an important part of America's maritime history.

By 1820 schooners outnumbered all other types of vessels in Maine. The early schooners generally carried square topsails on the foremast, hence, "topsail schooner." A vessel rigged fore-and-aft only was known as a "fore-and-after."

The greatest assets of the fore-and-aft rig were its windward ability, ease of sail handling, and the small crews needed to safely manage it. Schooners were not only handy, but they could be built easily and economically using local materials and labor.

Small two- and three-masted schooners were the errand boys of the coast and could be found in every river and bay. Their weatherliness rendered them independent of tugboats when entering and leaving port. They carried farm products, hay, lumber, dried fish, bricks, lime, ice, and granite from Maine to the southern cities of the East Coast. In turn they brought back southern pine, pitch, tar, oak ship timbers, turpentine, salt, manufactured goods, tools, and general merchandise. The coastal schooners that sailed along shores of New England not only carried the commerce of the region, but also served as the training vessels for the seamen that formed the basis of the American merchant marine.

By 1870, the rapid expansion of New England industries and the growth of railroad service meant large quantities of coal for steam power had to be shipped north from the Chesapeake. At the same time, competition from foreign-built steel vessels, for transoceanic trade, reduced orders for the large square-rigged "Down Easters" that were being built in Maine's major shipyards. These factors encouraged shipbuilders to strive for larger carrying capacities in coastal schooners. It should be noted that America's coastal shipping routes have been protected from foreign vessels since an act of Congress in 1789.

The fore-and-aft schooner was kept alive, chiefly in the state of Maine, by expanding the size of the vessel. These larger schooners not only met the need to move greater quantities of cargo, but also kept the large shipyards in operation.

When the three-masters of the 1870s had been pushed to capacity in hull design and tonnage, a fourth mast was added and the hull expanded. By adding another mast, the sail area on each mast could be kept relatively smaller than if the size of the sail alone had been increased. The resulting shorter booms were less hazardous when carried outboard in a heavy sea. Even the larger vessels could be managed by relatively small crews from the decks, making the rig easier to handle and, therefore, more profitable than the square-rigged vessels.

In 1888, the first five-masted schooner, the *Governor Ames*, was launched in Waldoboro, Maine. The *Governor Ames* was the largest schooner to be built with a centerboard. The board measured 35 feet in length. By 1920, 52 five-masters had been built in Maine.

In 1900, the first six-masted schooner, the *George W. Wells*, was launched in Camden. Nine wooden six-masted vessels were built, all in Maine.

The last and greatest of the giant wooden schooners was the six-masted *Wyoming*, built at the Percy and Small Shipyard in Bath, Maine, in 1909. The *Wyoming* was one of the largest wooden sailing vessels of any rig ever built. She registered 3,730 gross tons and was 329.5 feet long, had a 50.1 foot beam and drew over 30 feet.

These large schooners, however, were not practical for wooden construction. The extreme length could not take the tremendous stress created by the alternating troughs and crests of the ocean's swells. A wooden vessel also has the inherent characteristic of its full mid-section having a greater buoyancy than its heavier ends, thus the ends tend to drop lower than the center. Such a vessel is said to be "hogged." In an attempt to remedy these problems, the vessels were built with a keelson of tremendous depth to strengthen their backbone. A large sheer also helped to conceal the effects of hogging and kept the poop and forecastle decks drier when the vessels were fully loaded.

In a desire to overcome the weakness and limitations of the large wooden hulls, shipbuilders began to experiment with steel in the construction of schooners. The steel-hulled seven-masted schooner *Thomas W. Lawson*, built in Massachusetts, was the ultimate in over-stretching the fore-and-aft rig. The largest of the schooners, she measured 395 feet long, had a 52 foot beam and drew 32 feet. The rigging alone for each mast on this giant weighed three tons; however, she could carry over 8,100 tons of cargo. Still, her length-to-breadth ratio of 7 to 1 was out of keeping with her rig. Although capable of sailing to windward, she was difficult—and sometimes impossible—to tack in moderate weather. In her aim to be the ultimate in economy, she had lost that virtue that had made the fore-and-aft schooner so successful—manageability.

The building of large coastal schooners fell into a depression around 1910. Ironically, the coal trade that had made them so profitable was a factor in their decline. As the demand for coal grew, the faster, more dependable steam fleets were increased to carry the load. Ocean-going tugs hauled long strings of barges loaded with coal. A few of these barges were cut-down schooners.

World War I touched off a new flurry of shipbuilding in America. Foreign countries withdrew their steel ships from commerce and put them to their own use in the war effort. America was forced to replace the foreign vessels with large old schooners. Once again the schooners were profitable and Maine shipbuilders came to life. The building of large schooners lasted until 1920, when the building of steam-driven steel ships caught up with America's needs. By the mid-1930s many of the schooners that were still trading on the coast became victims of the depression. A few small, worn-out schooners carried pulpwood to the paper mills, but the commercial schooner was dying out.

From its beginning, the fore-and-aft rig proved to be extremely versatile and was adapted to many different types of working vessels. The history of the coasters has been discussed, but there were other vessels designed to be used in the

New England fisheries and mid-Atlantic oyster dredging industry. Much of the East Coast's fortune lay in the ocean's depths. To bring these riches to market required the best of Yankee shipbuilding ingenuity.

The knockabout Gloucester fishing schooners were the epitome of a refined fore-and-aft rig. Their deep keel, fine lines, and tall rig made them swift and seaworthy. These graceful fishing vessels were built to take the gales of the North Atlantic off Georges Bank and the Grand Bank. Carrying their nests of fishing dories, they were capable of remaining at sea for extended periods of time, then returned to port with great speed to sell their catches. Smaller versions of the knockabout design were used in seining for the sardine fisheries.

Another adaptation of the fore-and-aft rig was the ram. These three-masted cargo schooners sailed primarily in the waters of the mid-Atlantic states. The rams were stoutly built vessels designed in two types. The "outside rams" traveled the outer coastal routes of the eastern seaboard, while the "inside rams" worked the inner waterways of the Chesapeake and Delaware Bays. The beam of the "inside rams" was within inches of the width of the C & D Canal.

Oyster dredging on the large bays of the mid-Atlantic required strong vessels that were capable of moving well in light air. Until the mid 1940s, law required that dredging for oysters be done under sail to prevent overworking the beds.

The heavy dredges that gathered the oysters by scraping them from the bottom were like anchors being dragged along by the schooner. When there was little wind and the dredges held fast, no catch could be made. Light air schooners could keep working and return to port quickly to sell their harvest.

The schooner rig was also used in pilot vessels. The pilot schooners were ruggedly built to withstand the rigors of remaining on their stations in open water, in all weather. These schooners carried the harbor pilots to the ships waiting at sea. The pilot was transferred to the ship in a small rowing boat. Once on board, the pilot guided the ship into port. For years the pilots were paid on a first-come basis. Competition at major ports could be brisk, forcing some schooners to sail many miles to sea so that their pilot would be the first to reach an incoming ship.

The small Maine coasting schooners carried many types

of cargo. From early spring until the freeze-up in the late fall, every vessel available along the mid-coast carried cordwood to the lime kilns in Rockland, Thomaston, and Rockport. At one time the kilns numbered well over 100, each one using an average of 30 cords of wood at each burning. Very often the cordwood was piled so high on the decks of a vessel that the helmsman could not see over it, and steering was directed by a man stationed forward on top of the load who shouted instructions aft. Many of these vessels were so old and leaky that their load of wood actually helped keep them afloat. These coasters had served their masters well and were now at the end of their careers. The average schooner, built along the coast, was not expected to last much over 15 years; however, many smaller ones were still working 30 to 50 years after they were launched.

In contrast to the schooners that carried the wood to the kilns, it was essential that the two-masters carrying lime kept their cargo dry. Water and lime had to be kept apart at all times for fear of fire caused by the chemical reaction when the two substances combined. If the lime did catch fire, it could not be extinguished, as water would only increase the blaze. The only hope of saving the vessel was to seal the hatches and starve the fire of air.

Granite quarrying was one of Maine's leading industries for many years. Both large and small schooners were used to carry the stone from island quarries to the southern cities for paving and buildings. In 1889, the city of Brooklyn, New York ordered eleven million paving blocks to be shipped from Maine over a period of a year. Courthouses, post offices, custom houses, and train stations were often built with Maine granite.

The life of a coaster captain in the late 19th and early 20th centuries was a challenging experience. Competition was strong and the work was hard but satisfying; an independent, aggressive skipper could do quite well. The masters of large schooners were remarkable seamen and navigators. It was no easy task to handle a big schooner along the crowded waterways of the Atlantic coast.

For the captains of the smaller vessels that worked the waters of northern New England, the winter freeze-ups meant they could either spend several months at home or sail on larger vessels to the West Indies.

After 1920 the returns for a coaster captain were meager. The coastal trade was waning, and often cargo could be found for only one way. Little profit was gained unless a return trip was also booked. Fog, storms, and ill winds could cause costly delays, leaving the money to venturesome young captains who took chances.

The captains of the coastal schooners did not enjoy the same privileges as those on larger craft. On the offshore vessels, routine sailing was left to the mates; often the captain exercised his command only in emergencies. The small coasters required the captain not only be on duty but also do his share of the work.

In 1938, the *Endeavor*, the last of the cargo schooners, was launched in Maine. The advent of better roads and other means of power brought an end to the days when Maine's harbors and bays were filled with schooners. Coastwise trade was reduced to a fraction of the volume that had been hauled just a few years earlier. All but a few of the remaining schooners were tied up to rot at the wharves.

A man named Frank Swift was inspired by these schooners. His desire to carry people on summer cruises was to give many of the old vessels a reprieve. Born in New York, Swift came to Maine as a boy. His great uncle had been a harpooner on a whaling ship in the mid 1800s—a fact which Swift claims gave him a nautical heritage. As a young man, Swift learned silversmithing and studied to be an artist. He loved the sea, though, and became a cadet on the *Newport*, New York State's school ship. By the age of 20, Swift was an able-bodied seaman and quartermaster aboard a steamship carrying case oil to Hong Kong, Hawaii and the Philippines.

In the mid 1930s he and his wife moved to East Orland, Maine. It was during the Depression, and making ends meet as an artist was not easy. He watched the pulpwood coasters sailing into Bucksport and wondered why they couldn't carry people. He explained his idea to Captain Parker Hall of Stockton Springs, who suggested he try to charter the 54-foot schooner, *Mabel*. Swift talked Captain Shepard of Deer Isle into going as her captain, and Mrs. Shepard agreed to cook. On that first trip in 1936, they carried only three passengers, and on the next cruise they sailed without any. Meanwhile, Swift chartered the 58-foot *Lydia M. Webster*.

The following summer the Swifts did fairly well carrying passengers on both vessels; however, Captain Swift was having doubts about the potential of the windjammer business. He decided to give it one more year, and added the *Annie F. Kimball* to the fleet—the first vessel he owned himself. After caulking, rerigging, and adding cabins for passengers, he took the *Annie F. Kimball* to Camden. During its third season the business caught on. Those first windjammer cruises cost $35.00 for the week.

Over the years Captain Swift used many vessels in his windjammer fleet, including *Mabel, Lydia M. Webster, Annie F. Kimball, Mattie, Clinton, Lois M. Candage, Eva S. Cullison, Enterprise, Yankee, Lillian,* and *Mercantile*. At one period he had nine schooners carrying passengers on weekly cruises. One of Swift's favorite vessels was the *Lois M. Candage*, which he skippered for seven years. The *Mattie* was favored by many of his passengers, and today she is still carrying return passengers who sailed on her when Swift was owner.

Captain Swift sold his windjammer business to Captain Jim Nisbet in 1961. Eight years later Captain Les Bex purchased the two remaining schooners from Swift's fleet, the *Mattie* and the *Mercantile*. Since the 1930s other captains have been carrying passengers for hire along the coast of Maine, and today there are many schooners involved in the business. These commercial vessels sail out of Rockland, Rockport, Camden, and Belfast—the same ports commercial schooners have worked for centuries. Several vessels in today's windjammer fleet have been designed and built exclusively to carry passengers, carrying on the heritage of Maine's shipbuilders into the 21st century.

24

Schooners under winter cover in
Camden Harbor.

LEWIS R. FRENCH

Tonnage	**50 gross tons**
Length on deck	**64 feet**
Beam	**19 feet**
Draft (full keel)	**7 feet 6 inches**
Sail area	**2,900 square feet**
Passengers	**22**
Crew	**4**

The *Lewis R. French* is a Maine coasting schooner built in Christmas Cove, Maine by the French Brothers in 1871. She is the oldest vessel in the Maine fleet, having been launched several months before the *Stephen Taber*. Both vessels hold their own distinction as to age however, and both are prime examples of the skill used in the art of shipbuilding in the late 19th century.

The *Lewis R. French* was built to carry general freight—including salt fish, lime, and coal—between Maine and Gloucester, Massachusetts. In 1877, the schooner was bought by a Boothbay group and used as a seiner until 1881, when she was returned to the coastal trade.

In 1928, while in Belfast harbor, a small engine exploded on board, blowing the caulk out of her seams sinking the

schooner as she burned. When she was raised, the *Lewis R. French* was fitted with a power plant and a single spar and used as a coasting vessel out of Vinalhaven carrying lumber and coal. In 1934 she was taken Downeast to serve as a cannery lighter carrying supplies to the sardine canneries.

Her present owner and captain, John Foss, bought her in 1973 and brought the vessel to Rockland, Maine. Raised in Freeport, Maine, Captain Foss had worked in boatyards during the summers as a boy. In 1968 he worked on the restoration of the *Bowdoin*. The following year he crewed on the *Adventure* until joining the Coast Guard. Over the years Captain Foss has worked on the restoration and repair of many vessels. Captain Foss saw the potential in the *Lewis R. French*, and in partnership with the Lees in both the vessel and the North End Shipyard, he spent the next two and one half years restoring the schooner. The restoration was extensive, using native oak and pine to replace timbers from the keel up, being careful to preserve the lines and charm of the original vessel.

In 1976, the *Lewis R. French* was launched as a schooner again, rebuilt to carry passengers in the cruise trade. Under Captain Foss's care, the *Lewis R. French* has been kept as strong and safe as the day she was built over a century ago. He is constantly refining her to keep her the fastest schooner in her class. The thrill of racing across the bay in the *Lewis R. French* will be experienced by only a few, but for a week or two during the summer, those few will come from far and wide to step aboard this historic vessel for a spirited sail into the past.

Schooner LEWIS R. FRENCH
entering Rockland Harbor.

STEPHEN TABER

Tonnage	41 gross tons
Length on deck	68 feet
Beam	22 feet 6 inches
Draft	5 feet
(centerboard down)	14 feet
Sail area	3,000 square feet
Passengers	22
Crew	5

The *Stephen Taber* is a fore-and-aft coasting schooner built in Glenwood Landing on Long Island, New York, in 1871. She is the oldest documented sailing vessel in continuous service in the United States. The *Stephen Taber* was originally designed to carry bricks on Long Island Sound and up the Hudson River. In the 1930s she was rebuilt on Verona Island, Maine to carry pulpwood from the offshore islands to the paper mills in Bucksport and Brewer.

In 1946, the *Stephen Taber* was purchased by Captain Frederick B. Guild and converted to carry passengers. An impressive number of windjammer captains have begun their careers as both captains and owners of the *Stephen Taber*. The

schooner's masters include Captains Guild, Hawkins, Sharp, Young, Anderson, and her present owner, Ken Barnes. Almost everyone who has become involved with the windjammer business in Maine has sailed on her at one time.

"Everyone owns the *Stephen Taber*." Captain Barnes informed me. "Any work that is done on her I must answer for to them all."

In the fall of 1981 Ken Barnes and his wife, Ellen, moved the *Stephen Taber* to the North End Shipyard in Rockland to undergo an extensive overhaul to insure her longevity.

The Barneses first sailed on the *Lewis R. French* and fell in love with windjammers and the coast of Maine.

"I found the days of sail were still alive," Captain Barnes said. "History could be lived."

They returned home and set up a schedule for moving to Maine and purchasing a schooner.

"We were lucky." Captain Barnes told me. "The *Stephen Taber* was for sale. We grabbed her."

The Barneses join the group of schooner owners who were introduced to the business as passengers or deck hands and just couldn't leave the sea.

The *Stephen Taber*, like most of the schooners, is family owned and operated. Everyone works on the vessel at some time or another. Captain Barnes sails the schooner while Ellen runs the galley.

The vessel is in good hands with the Barneses. This small schooner that has played such a vital role in the growth of the windjammer fleet will continue to introduce people to the romance of the sea by making them members of her "crew."

Schooner STEPHEN TABER on
Penobscot Bay.

MATTIE

Tonnage	**59 gross tons**
Length on deck	**80 feet**
Beam	**23 feet 6 inches**
Draft	**7 feet**
(centerboard down)	**11 feet 6 inches**
Sail area	**3,622 square feet**
Passengers	**29**
Crew	**5**

The *Mattie* is a gaff-rigged coastal schooner built by Oliver Perry Smith at his boatyard in Patchogue, New York in 1882. The vessel was built for E. Bailey and Sons Lumber Co. to carry lumber from ports in the south, and was originally named the *Grace Bailey* after Edwin Bailey's daughter. However, in 1906 when the vessel was rebuilt, it was renamed after Bailey's 18-year-old granddaughter, *Mattie*.

The *Mattie* carried lumber and foreign trade as far as the West Indies until 1914. She was then moved to New Haven, Connecticut, where she was used to carry oysters on Long Island Sound. During this time she had a double topsail rig.

In 1920 the schooner was brought to Belfast, Maine by Captain Black of South Brooksville, Maine. The *Mattie* was to replace the schooner *Oakwoods*, which had been accidentally rammed and sunk by an American submarine in Buzzards Bay. The United States Government paid Captain Black for his loss, but the check was never cashed. Years after his death the check was discovered hidden over a beam in the *Mattie's* master cabin. The schooner was used as a Maine coaster carrying pulpwood, coal, hardwood, and cod. She also carried Maine granite from Crotch Island to New York City for the building of the Post Office and Grand Central Station.

In 1939, Captain Frank Swift chartered the *Mattie* as an addition to his fleet of cruise schooners. The following year he purchased the vessel and converted her to carry passengers. During the summer of 1942 she was chartered by the Maine Maritime Academy as its first training vessel. With that brief exception, she has sailed continuously as a cruise schooner under the ownership of Captains Swift, Nisbet, and Bex.

The *Mattie* is now commanded by Captain Ted Schmidt. In 1966 Captain Schmidt came to New England from Ohio for a sail on the *Mattie*. The following year he returned for a second ride, and then he crewed on the schooner for two weeks. The next summer he was asked to crew again and signed on as cook. He cooked for three years, followed by six years on deck. In 1977 he took over as captain of the *Mattie*.

Captain Schmidt feels that if his passengers depart with a richer understanding of nature and an appreciation for a slower pace of life, he and his crew have been successful.

Schooner MATTIE off Mark
Island.

ISAAC H. EVANS

Tonnage	52 gross tons
Length on deck	65 feet
Beam	20 feet
Draft	6 feet
(centerboard down)	14 feet
Sail area	2,600 square feet
Passengers	22
Crew	4

The *Isaac H. Evans* is a Delaware Bay oyster dragger schooner built in Mauricetown, New Jersey, in 1886. Originally named the *Boyd N. Shepard*, the schooner was built with a life expectancy of some 20 years as part of the oystering fleet. In 1919, 25 years after her launching, she was bought by the Evans brothers, who rebuilt her, added an auxiliary engine, and renamed her after their father, *Isaac H. Evans*. The vessel was kept in service until 1933 when the Depression took its toll on many industries. That year the *Isaac H. Evans* was beached in a mud creek alongside several other craft, and sunk. The mud covering the schooner protected the timbers from fresh water, preserving the hull.

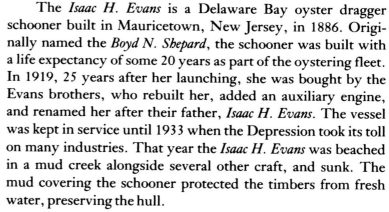

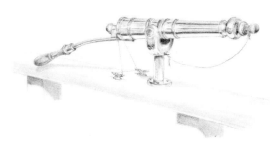

In 1936, the *Isaac H. Evans* was dug out of the mud, re-topped with new deck timbers, and put back into the oystering trade. When the law allowing full-power dredging was enacted in 1946, the schooner was dismasted and a pilot house added on deck. In 1954, the first of several tragedies hit the *Isaac H. Evans*. A gas pier to which she was docked caught fire, and the vessel was nearly lost. Extensive repairs had to be made before she was able to dredge again. Twelve years later, in 1966, ice ripped out one of her planks and she sank. Raised and again repaired, she continued oystering until 1971, when Doug and Linda Lee bought her. The Lees took the *Isaac H. Evans* to the Percy and Small Shipyard in Bath, Maine, hauled her out, and worked two years rebuilding and rerigging the schooner for the cruise trade. On July 12, 1973, the rebuilt *Isaac H. Evans* was launched as the beautiful, solid, Coast Guard approved vessel she is today. Later that month, the Lees sailed the *Isaac H. Evans* out of Rockland, Maine, with a full passenger list.

Since that date, Captains Doug and Linda Lee have restored several old schooners and are now building a new 93-foot schooner named *Heritage* at their North End Shipyard in Rockland. On shore, the two work hand in hand, setting timbers, fastening planks, and caulking seams. At sea, Doug charts their course and handles the vessel, while Linda prepares piping hot food that will satisfy any seafarer's appetite.

Sailing on the *Isaac H. Evans* is like sailing with friends who make a genuine effort to help you enjoy your stay, and as each day goes by, you realize you are living a portion of America's history aboard a vessel that helped shape that history.

40

Schooner ISAAC EVANS on
Jericho Bay.

VICTORY CHIMES

Tonnage	208 gross tons
Length on deck	132 feet
Beam	24 feet
Draft	8 feet 4 inches
(centerboard down)	19 feet
Sail area	5,984 square feet
Passengers	46
Crew	9

The *Victory Chimes* is a three-masted schooner built in Bethel, Delaware in 1900. She was designed as a ram and was originally named the *Edwin and Maud*. Built to carry cargo on the Chesapeake Bay, where she was owned for many years, the schooner also hauled lumber from the Carolinas to Philadelphia, New York, and other eastern seaboard ports.

The *Victory Chimes* is constructed of heavy Georgian pine and live oak, fastened with galvanized iron. Her masts tower 80 feet above her decks, and her beam is just inches less than the 24-foot width of the Delaware and Chesapeake canal. It is believed that these stout schooners were called rams because they were built with the strength of early military vessels which rammed their enemies as a defense.

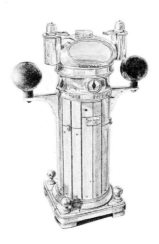

For almost 50 years the *Victory Chimes* earned her way freighting along the eastern seaboard. In 1954, Captain Frederick B. Guild and a group of associates purchased the schooner. Captain Guild renamed her *Victory Chimes* and brought her to the Maine coast.

Captain Guild came from a sailing family. As a small boy he sailed on Martha's Vineyard. In 1932, he began carrying passengers along the Maine coast with a 38-foot Friendship sloop. During the winter of 1933 he sailed as second mate aboard the five-masted schooner *Edna Hoyt*. Six years later he purchased the 48-foot Friendship sloop *Georgie C. Bowden*.

In 1942, Captain Guild joined the U.S. Coast Guard, where he served as a commanding officer in the Corsair fleet. After the war, Captain Guild and his wife Janet resumed their vacation cruise business, first with the *Georgie C. Bowden*, then with the schooners *Stephen Taber* and *Alice S. Wentworth*, both of which they had converted to the cruise trade.

In 1959 the Guilds purchased the *Victory Chimes* outright and began a complete overhaul of the schooner. Today she is a proud example of a well-run vessel, agleam with brass and brightwork, and operated with pride and the strictest traditions of seamanship. Each heated stateroom has hot and cold running water. A professional cook presides over the galley. In the forward deckhouse the donkey engine, built in 1916, provides power for the anchor windlass. Sailing on the *Victory Chimes* is an enriching experience, combining a relaxing vacation with the polish of a beautiful vessel and a disciplined crew.

Schooner VICTORY CHIMES
off Porterfield Ledge.

SYLVINA W. BEAL

Tonnage	44 gross tons
Length on deck	78 feet
Beam	17 feet 1 inch
Draft (full keel)	7 feet 11 inches
Sail area	2,500 square feet
Passengers	18
Crew	4

The *Sylvina W. Beal* is a two-masted schooner built at the Frank Adams Yard in East Boothbay, Maine in 1910. The vessel, constructed of native oak, was built for Charles Henry Beal and named after his wife.

Designed as a sardine carrier, the *Sylvina W. Beal* transported the herring catch from the netting-off dories to port. She was less beamy and lighter than the coasting schooners, both because her 70 hogsheads of fish were a comparatively light cargo and to increase her speed.

The *Sylvina W. Beal* first served the Peacock Canneries at Eastport and later the Stinson plants along the Maine coast. Although she had a small auxiliary engine, by the mid 1930s the increased use of power boats made her too slow to be profitable. To keep pace, she was dismasted, a pilot house was added, and

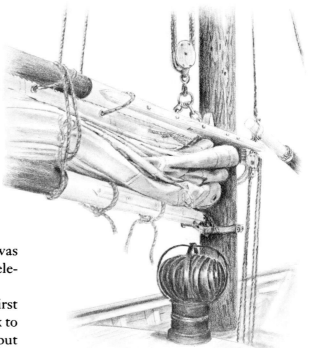

she was fitted with two large engines. Still, the small vessel was no match for the large power boats and she was eventually relegated to carrying bait.

In the late 1950s the *Sylvina W. Beal* was sold to the first of several parties, each of whom wanted to convert her back to sail but lacked the funds. Finally, the vessel was seized and put up for auction to pay off her yard bills.

Captain John Worth and his wife, Trish, had been looking for a windjammer. When they heard of the sale, they researched the vessel and decided to try to acquire her. Captain Worth had been sailing on the bay for over eight years and was then captain of the schooner *Mercantile*.

When the auction was over, they owned the *Sylvina W. Beal*. He took the vessel to a yard in Southwest Harbor, removed the 9-foot-high pilot house, replaced the two large engines with a smaller single engine, and repaired the outer hull. On a brisk autumn day in 1980, he motored the bare hull to Belfast. For the next nine months, during the cold Maine winter, Captain Worth, Trish, both of their families, and several friends rebuilt the *Sylvina W. Beal*, converting her back to her original sailing rig and fitting her out to carry passengers.

"It was a labor of love." Captain Worth told me. "The whole family pitched in, doing everything from carpentry work to sewing mattresses."

In June of 1981 the *Sylvina W. Beal* left Belfast on her maiden voyage as a cruise schooner. Once again, she was sailing where she belonged among the coastal islands of Maine.

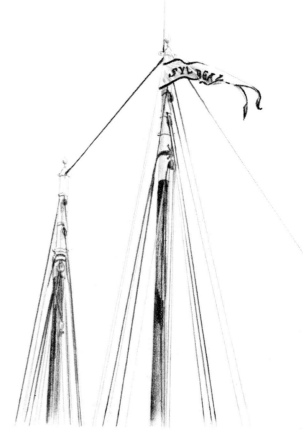

48

Schooner SYLVINA W. BEAL
off Turtle Head.

MERCANTILE

Tonnage	**47 gross tons**
Length on deck	**80 feet**
Beam	**22 feet**
Draft	**6 feet 7 inches**
(centerboard down)	**10 feet 7 inches**
Sail area	**3,015 square feet**
Passengers	**26**
Crew	**5**

The *Mercantile* is a gaff-rigged coastal schooner, built by the Billings family on Little Deer Isle, Maine, in 1916. She was one of five coasters built by the Billings with lumber cut on the site. A piece of apple tree with a branch attached was used as a framing member in her bow. The vessels were built during the winter months when farming and other occupations could not be pursued.

Pearl Billings, one of the builders, was the first of several members of the family to own and master the *Mercantile*. The schooner was built with a shoal draft, making her capable of taking on and discharging cargo in small, shallow harbors. She carried many different cargoes, including firewood for the lime kilns in Rockport, Maine, and salt fish from Swan's Island to Gloucester, Massachusetts.

In 1939, the *Mercantile* collided with a steamer while they attempted to pass at night on the Penobscot River. The schooner received considerable damage to her bow and was towed by the steamer to Bucksport, where her cargo of pulpwood was unloaded. When the Maine coasting trade died off in the early 1940s, the *Mercantile* was sold to Captain Charles O'Connor of Warwick, Rhode Island, who used the vessel as a mackerel fisher on Narragansett Bay.

In 1942 the *Mercantile* was purchased by Captain Frank Swift of Camden, Maine. He added her to his fleet of cruise schooners, which at the time consisted of the *Clinton*, *Mattie*, *Lois M. Candage*, *Lillian*, *Eva S. Cullison*, and the *Enterprise*. Of that fleet only the *Mattie* and the *Mercantile* remain.

After Captain Swift, the *Mercantile* was owned by Captain Jim Nisbet and is presently owned by Captain Les Bex.

It is a credit to Yankee craftsmanship that the *Mercantile*, which was built with the intention of serving only a few years, still survives after almost 70 years. Each week during the summer she carries passengers to many of the same ports where she once carried cargo. Her holds are now staterooms, and on her decks, where bricks and lumber were once piled, passengers relax and enjoy the wonders of nature. Whether it be an arctic tern skimming across the water, a great blue heron flying overhead, or a giant whale surfacing a few yards from the rail, the experiences will long be remembered.

Sailing on the *Mercantile* is stepping back in time aboard a living example of Maine's maritime heritage.

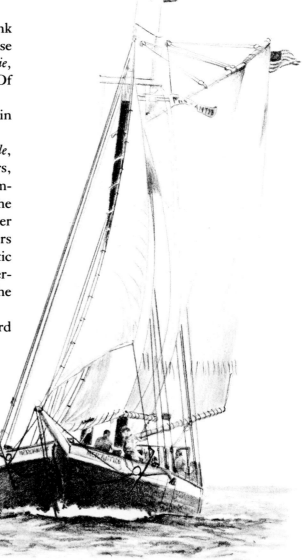

Schooner MERCANTILE in
Eggemoggin Reach.

BOWDOIN

Tonnage	66 gross tons
Length on deck	88 feet
Beam	21 feet
Draft (full keel)	10 feet
Sail area	2,900 square feet
Passengers	12
Crew	4

The *Bowdoin* is a knockabout Grand Banks schooner built at the Hodgdon Brothers Shipyard in East Boothbay, Maine, in 1921. Designed by William Hand to specifications determined by Rear Admiral Donald B. MacMillan, she was to be used in Arctic exploration. MacMillan first sailed to the Arctic in 1908 with Admiral Peary. During the next 10 years he planned the new schooner by studying the design of vessels that became trapped in the ice and crushed. Constructed of native oak, the *Bowdoin's* sharp bilges and spoon-shaped, knockabout bow tended to raise the vessel up onto the closing masses of ice. To help protect her from the deadly sea ice floes the schooner has a five-foot belt of 1½-inch ironwood sheathing, a steel nose weighing 1,800 pounds, and over 21 tons of concrete and iron ballast. The schooner was powered by a 40-horsepower Fairbanks diesel auxiliary.

The *Bowdoin* made 26 voyages of exploration into the Arctic during which she was often frozen into the ice for months at a time. When the floes began to breakup, Admiral MacMillan would command the schooner through the polar ice from the ice barrel above the fore spreader.

During World War II the *Bowdoin* was used by the U.S. Army as a pilot ship on the west coast of Greenland.

In 1957, at the age of 83, MacMillan turned the *Bowdoin* over to Mystic Seaport in Connecticut. Ten years later the schooner was moved to Camden, Maine, by a group called the Schooner *Bowdoin* Association and leased to Captain Jim Sharp to be put into sailing condition. For the next several years she was sailed along the Maine coast. In 1976, the association became a non-profit educational group called Schooner *Bowdoin* Inter-Island Expeditions. Under the command of Captain John Nugent, the *Bowdoin* was used as a teaching vessel, taking people on educational cruises. Courses in marine biology, navigation, and maritime history were taught from her decks.

In 1979, the *Bowdoin* was taken to the Goudy and Stevens Shipyard in East Boothbay, Maine to undergo extensive restoration. Later, she was moved to the Percy and Small Shipyard in Bath to be used as a focus for the Maine Maritime Museum's shipwright training program. Financed by a grant and private donations, the *Bowdoin* will soon be restored to her original strength and lines. The schooner will continue as a seagoing school and research vessel and perhaps return to the Arctic.

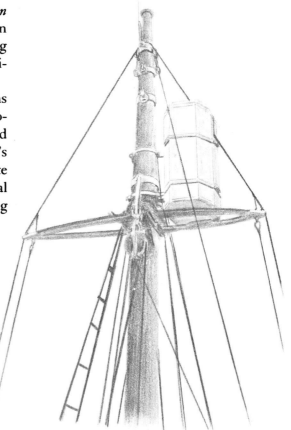

Schooner BOWDOIN off Deer
Island.

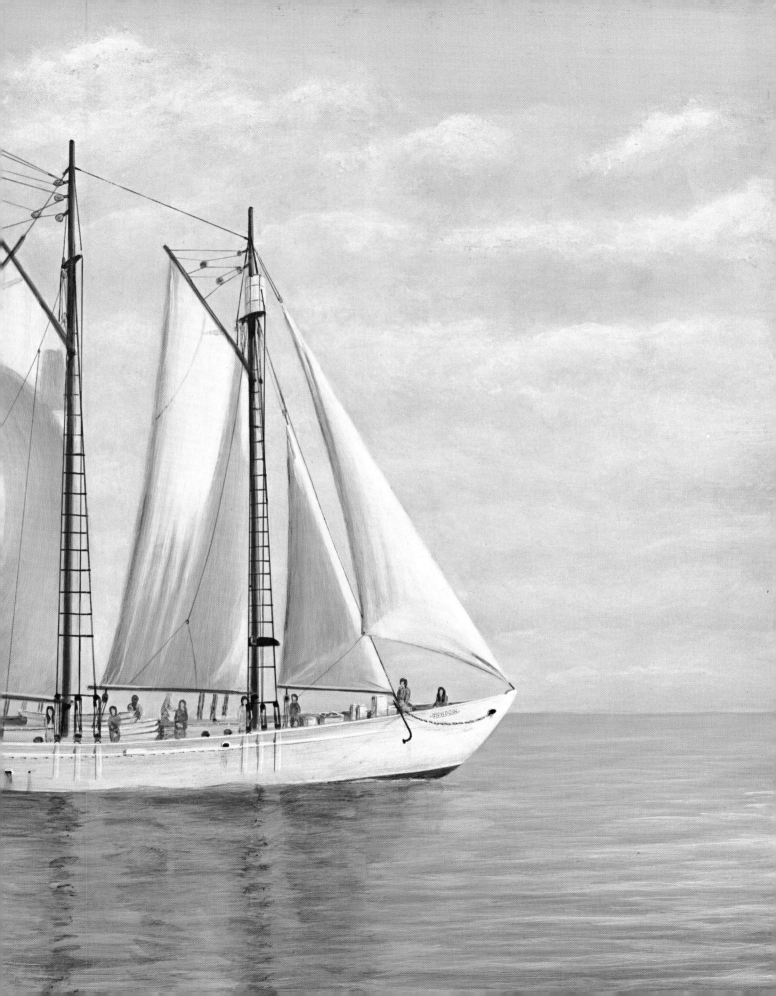

NATHANIEL BOWDITCH

Tonnage	90 gross tons
Length on deck	82 feet
Beam	21 feet 6 inches
Draft (full keel)	11 feet
Sail area	3,700 square feet
Passengers	24
Crew	4

The *Nathaniel Bowditch* is a fore-and-aft gaff-rigged schooner built in the Hodgdon Brothers Shipyard in East Boothbay, Maine, in 1923. Originally named the *Ladonna*, she is a sister ship to the *Bowdoin*, which was built in the same yard a year earlier. The vessel was designed by William Hand as a racing schooner for Homer Loring of Boston. In 1924, she finished first overall in the Bermuda Race. Later, she was renamed the *Jane Dore* and used as a private yacht sailing out of the New York Yacht Club.

During World War II the schooner served on antisubmarine patrol as part of the Coast Guard Corsair fleet. After the war, she was converted to a dragger on Long Island Sound and became a highliner of the fishing fleet. In the early 1960s the schooner was purchased by Bob Douglas, who took her to Martha's Vineyard. In 1967, she was brought to Stonington,

Maine, by Skip Hawkins and renamed the *Joseph W. Hawkins*. Hawkins began to rebuild the vessel at the Billings Yard in Stonington with hopes of adding her to the windjammer fleet; however, these plans did not materialize. In 1971, she was sold to Roger Brainerd and Carl Chase, who called their charter company the American Practical Navigators Inc. after the famous book on navigation. They renamed the schooner the *Nathaniel Bowditch* in honor of the book's author. The two men rebuilt the schooner and used her as a training vessel.

In 1975, her present owner, Captain Gib Philbrick, bought the *Nathaniel Bowditch* in partnership with Kip Leach. Captain Philbrick installed staterooms for passengers and began sailing her on week-long cruises out of Rockland, Maine.

Captain Philbrick was raised in northern Maine and worked many years as a guide in the north woods. Later, he spent the summers skippering a 48-foot staysail schooner out of Bucks Harbor. He sailed the vessel and cooked for eight passengers on weekly cruises.

"Sailing the *Nathaniel Bowditch* is like being a form of guide again." Captain Philbrick told me. "It's a special type of vacation for a special type of person."

Life aboard the *Nathaniel Bowditch* is easygoing and informal. Each week's cruise is different, for the wind and weather determine where the schooner will go. The food is excellent and the adventure unforgettable as you enjoy the romance of sail and the beauty of Maine.

Schooner NATHANIEL
BOWDITCH on Isle Au Haut
Bay.

62

Great Schooner Race off North
Haven.

ROSEWAY

Tonnage	97.4 gross tons
Length on deck	112 feet
Beam	25 feet
Draft (full keel)	12 feet 9 inches
Sail area	5,000 square feet
Passengers	36
Crew	7

The *Roseway* is a fore-and-aft schooner built at the James Yard in Essex, Massachusetts in 1925. Although she was designed as a private yacht for Judge Hathaway of Boston, her lines follow those of a Gloucester fisherman. Her hull is almost 18 inches thick, constructed of blue-white oak hand-picked from a stand in Taunton, Massachusetts. In 1941 she was sold to the Boston Pilots and commissioned as a pilot schooner. The *Roseway* carried the pilots to ships waiting offshore. The pilots were then transferred to incoming ships to guide them safely into Boston Harbor. On one trip the schooner was dismasted in a storm that packed winds of over 70 knots. The crew dropped both anchors and sent out a May Day. Shortly afterward, the Coast Guard removed those on board by helicopter,

and the *Roseway* was left to the mercy of the sea. After the storm, the *Roseway* was found sitting quietly at anchor, with not a drop of water in her bilge.

The *Roseway* remained a pilot schooner until 1972, when she was purchased by the Roseway Association to carry passengers on pleasure cruises. However, that project was abandoned in 1974 due to lack of funds. In 1975, Captains Jim Sharp and Orvil Young purchased the vessel, fitted her out, and sailed from Camden, Maine, that year carrying passengers.

The *Roseway* is distinguished by her tanbark sails, beautiful sheer, and inboard power. Captain Orvil Young, part owner and captain of the *Roseway*, has spent his life around boats and has been sailing schooners out of Camden since the mid-1960s. He first cruised with Captain Sharp on the *Stephen Taber*. In 1964 when Captain Sharp purchased the *Adventure*, Captain Young bought the *Stephen Taber* in partnership with Captain Sharp. The following year, his wife Andrea cooked for the passengers and crew. Andrea's meals were so well liked that she not only continued on as cook, but was asked to add many of her recipes to a windjammer cookbook. In 1974, Captain Sharp sold the *Stephen Taber* to Mike Anderson and the next year he bought the *Roseway*.

Captain Young is a genuine "Down Easter;" his relaxed nature and experienced hand, accompanied by Andrea's fine cooking, make sailing on the *Roseway* a true Maine experience.

The *Roseway* has represented the State of Maine in Operation Sail in both 1976 and 1979 and continues to represent the proud days of sail.

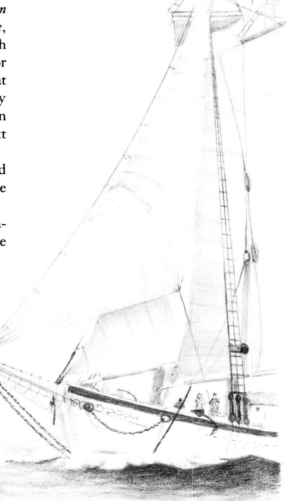

Schooner ROSEWAY in Mussel
Ridge Channel.

ADVENTURE

Tonnage	134 gross tons
Length on deck	121 feet
Beam	25 feet
Draft (full keel)	13 feet
Sail area	6,000 square feet
Passengers	37
Crew	7

The *Adventure* is a Gloucester fishing schooner, built in the James Yard in Essex, Massachusetts, in 1926. The Gloucester schooners were finely developed sailing vessels, built to take the severe North Atlantic gales with ease and speed. Designed by Thomas P. McManns, the *Adventure* is not only extremely fast but also graceful in lines and balance. Built of oak some 18 inches thick, the *Adventure's* lines were taken from the *Oretha F. Spinney*, the star of the film, *Captains Courageous*. Half a century later, in 1977, the *Adventure* starred in a television adaptation of the same story.

The *Adventure* began in 1926 under Captain Jeff Thomas, who died on board in 1934. That year Captain Leo Hynes became her new captain and remained so until 1953. Captain

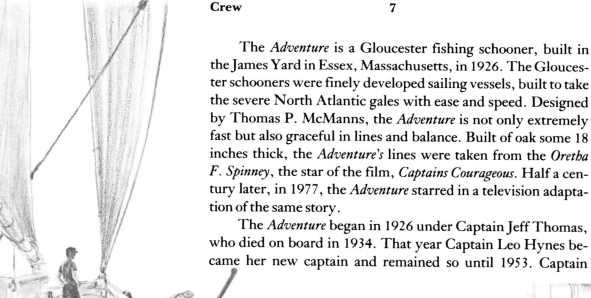

Hynes's career smashed all records in the fisheries, carrying stock totaling over 3.5 million dollars, and earning the schooner the nickname "Old Queen." The *Adventure* was truly a high-liner, and today is the only surviving member of a fleet of literally thousands of sailing fishermen.

In 1953 the schooner ended her days as a fisherman, and a few years later her fish pens were converted into cabins to carry passengers on long cruises. In 1964 the *Adventure* was purchased by her present owner, Captain Jim Sharp.

Captain Sharp was raised in Philadelphia. As a boy he boated on the Chesapeake Bay. Later, he owned several boats including a 45-foot yawl which he sailed from Florida to the Bahamas on charter. In 1957 Captain Sharp cruised on the *Adventure* as a passenger. In Florida, he met Captain Jim Nisbet, owner of the *Mattie* and *Mercantile*, who persuaded him to sail as mate on his vessels in Maine. Shortly thereafter Captain Sharp purchased the *Stephen Taber*.

In 1964, he moved to Maine and purchased the *Adventure*. That winter he completely gutted the schooner, building new spacious cabins, a companionway the length of her interior, and rerigging her to the original tall rig and sail area.

Today, the *Adventure* is once again the fastest member of the fleet, churning up the waters along the Maine coast and beyond. Her speed is well known, having won the Great Schooner Race for the past five years.

Whether you are racing under full sail, sitting in a quiet cove, or joining the captain in song in the main cabin, sailing on the *Adventure* is an unforgettable opportunity.

Schooner ADVENTURE in Fox
Island Thorofare.

J. & E. RIGGIN

Tonnage	61 gross tons
Length on deck	89 feet
Beam	22 feet 6 inches
Draft	7 feet
(centerboard down)	14 feet
Sail area	3,500 square feet
Passengers	26
Crew	5

The *J. & E. Riggin* is a Delaware Bay oyster dredging schooner, built in the Stowman Brothers Shipyard in Dorchester, New Jersey, in 1927. The vessel was built for Charles Riggin and named after his two sons, Jake and Ed. All three men captained the schooner at one time or another.

Built for oystering, the *J. & E. Riggin* was a proud member of the fleet. She was a light air vessel. Known as a "hanger on," she could continue working in only a slight breeze when the rest of the fleet was held at anchor by their dredges. Sailing wing-and-wing, she could return home faster than the other vessels with their push boats going. In 1929, she won the Delaware Bay Great Schooner Race.

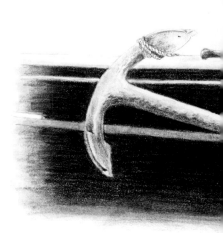

In the mid-'40s the *J. & E. Riggin* was sold to a party in Cape May, New Jersey, who removed her masts and converted her to a power dredge. In 1950, she was brought to Greenport, Long Island and used as a dragger in the mackerel fishing industry. She continued fishing until 1971, when David Lewis bought her and took her to Cape Cod to be used as a sailing museum. Lewis began to convert her back to a sailing schooner; however, he succeeded only as far as stripping her down.

In 1974, Captain Dave Allen and his wife Sue bought the bare hull and had it towed to Rockland, Maine. The voyage up the coast was an adventure through a November snowstorm. A full gale whipped up 20-foot seas as the tug pulled the hull northward to the North End Shipyard.

It took two-and-one-half years of hard work for the Allens to rebuild the *J. & E. Riggin* into a fully restored vessel fitted out to carry passengers. Working on schooners was old hat to Captain Allen though; as far back as he can remember his family has been around ships and the sea. His father captained the *Stephen Taber* and later the *Richard Robbins*, with David as a member of the crew.

Today, Captain Allen and Sue sail the *J. & E. Riggin* along the rugged coast of Maine, stopping each evening at a different harbor. Their passengers enjoy lobster bakes, walks on deserted islands, and strolls down the quiet streets of Down East fishing villages. Year after year, the Allens' love for their vessel, for people, and for the sea keep passengers coming back to relax and sail with them.

Schooner J. & E. RIGGIN off
Mark Island light.

TIMBERWIND

Tonnage	49 gross tons
Length on deck	70 feet
Beam	18 feet 6 inches
Draft (full keel)	9 feet 7 inches
Sail area	2,400 square feet
Passengers	20
Crew	5

The *Timberwind* is a two-masted pilot schooner built at Brown's Wharf in Portland, Maine, in 1931. The schooner was built by the Portland pilots themselves and served that harbor from 1931 until 1969. As a pilot schooner, the *Timberwind* carried the pilot captains to the vessels waiting at sea for safe entrance into the harbor. This required a stoutly built craft that could withstand most any weather. On one occasion, the *Timberwind* was forced to lay offshore for three days, waiting for the wind and seas to subside enough to return to port.

No matter what the conditions, the pilot had to be put aboard the waiting ship. The two vessels never rafted; rather, the pilot was transferred from one to the other in a small dory. This operation was especially dangerous at her station, 15 miles at sea near the Portland Light Ship. Yet in almost 40 years of

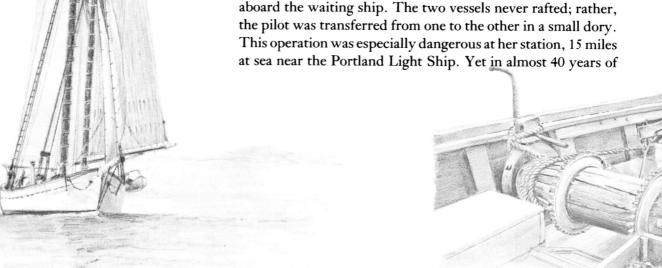

service, only one man was lost.

In 1969, the *Timberwind* was taken out of service. Later that year, Captain Bill Alexander, who had been searching for a vessel to use in the windjammer trade, convinced the Portland Pilot Association that he would care for the *Timberwind* and keep her in Maine waters.

"She was sitting at the wharf like a comfortable old shoe they hated to get rid of," he told me.

Captain Alexander brought the *Timberwind* to Rockport, removed her two large engines, and fitted her out to carry passengers. A year and a half later, in June of 1971 the schooner began her first cruise with Captain Alexander at the helm.

As a young man, Captain Alexander sailed a 19-foot sloop along the Jersey shore. Later, he spent his summers crewing on the *Mattie* and *Mercantile*. After receiving his captain's license, he charter-sailed the schooner *Mary E.* out of Rockland, Maine, before purchasing the *Timberwind*.

The *Timberwind* is a family operation; Captain Alexander's wife Julie hires the cooks, prepares the menu, keeps the records, and books the passengers. During the cold Maine winters, Bill Alexander is a high school teacher in Fairfield, Maine.

Captain Alexander describes the *Timberwind* as a small, intimate vessel with an enjoyable crew. She is easy to sail, yet heavily built and comfortable.

The *Timberwind* is a beautiful schooner with a proud Maine heritage. Her topsail rig and graceful sheer make any sailor take notice as she races across the bay.

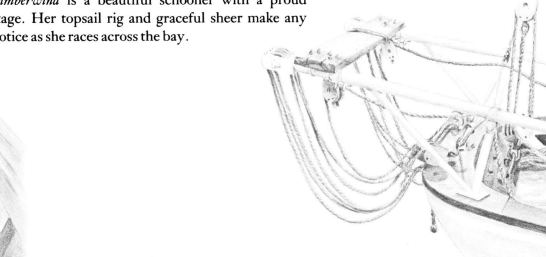

Schooner TIMBERWIND off
Indian Island Light.

MARY DAY

Tonnage	**86 gross tons**
Length on deck	**83 feet**
Beam	**23 feet 6 inches**
Draft	**7 feet**
(centerboard down)	**14 feet**
Sail area	**4,500 square feet**
Passengers	**28**
Crew	**5**

The *Mary Day* is a two-masted fore-and-aft schooner built by Harvey Gamage in the Gamage Shipyard in South Bristol, Maine, in 1961. The vessel was designed by her owner and captain, Havilah S. Hawkins. The *Mary Day* is the first coastal schooner to be designed and built exclusively to carry passengers. Her lines are those of a traditional schooner, but her accommodations are planned with comfort in mind. Below, the cabins have ample headroom, ventilation, and light, while on deck the low cabin tops allow good visibility from the helm.

Captain Hawkins has spent most of his life on the water. As a small boy in Greenwich Village in New York City, he dug a pond in the back yard, built a model schooner, filled it with tobacco pouches, then sailed the tiny craft from one side of the

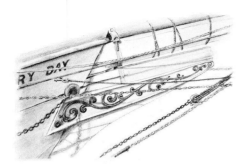

pond to the other and unloaded the cargo. He spent his summers in Maine where he loaded pulpwood on coastal schooners for 65 cents an hour.

"I've always wanted to own a coaster," he told me. "One summer I built a raft with a centerboard and a handmade wheel. Believe it or not, that raft would go to windward."

Pulled to the romance of the sea since childhood, Captain Hawkins's first schooner was the *Stephen Taber*, which he purchased from Captain Guild in 1950. Later, he also owned the *Alice Wentworth*, and in 1962 launched the *Mary Day*—a young boy's dream come true.

Most of the windjammer captains have been guided by Captain Hawkins at one time or another. "I try to encourage interested people who I think will be a credit to the business," he told me. A sailor, inventor, naval architect, and designer, Captain Hawkins has much to offer. On the *Mary Day* he can often be found near the helm telling stories or by the Franklin stove in the main cabin playing the fiddle.

The *Mary Day* has no onboard power, and water for drinking and washing is dipped from barrels on deck; however, these things lend to an atmosphere that helps one relax and see life.

Each captain is different, and therefore each vessel and each cruise is different. Captain Hawkins's love for the sea, people, music, and an easier pace, combined with the thrill of racing across the water aboard a fully rigged schooner, make sailing the coast of Maine on the *Mary Day* an experience that keeps people coming back year after year.

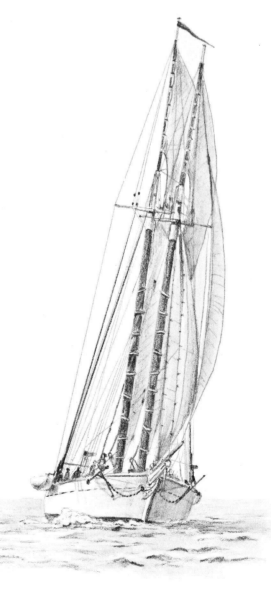

82

Schooner MARY DAY entering
Camden harbor.

MISTRESS

Tonnage	13 gross tons
Length on deck	40 feet
Beam	12 feet
Draft (full keel)	5 feet
Sail area	994 square feet
Passengers	6
Crew	2

The *Mistress* is a two-masted schooner begun on Deer Isle as a pleasure craft by a Mr. Eaton in 1960. The small vessel was a backyard project, designed to be used as a private yacht. Mr. Eaton worked on the hull intermittently for some time before it was purchased in 1966 by Captain Jim Nisbet and brought to Camden, Maine. The Nisbets completed the schooner, designing the interior to accomodate three couples in separate spacious cabins, each with its own head. When the *Mistress* was completed, Captain Nisbet added her to his other schooners being used to carry passengers on week-long cruises.

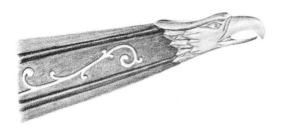

In 1969, the *Mistress* was sold to Captain Les Bex, along with the schooners *Mattie* and *Mercantile*. Captain Bex came to Maine in 1965 for a cruise on the *Mary Day*. Later, he signed on as member of the crew with Captain Hawkins. In 1968 he sailed on the *Mattie*. Captain Bex enjoys working with wood, and the challenge of a wooden windjammer seemed like a perfect outlet for him. The next spring he purchased Captain Nisbet's schooners. He had wanted a schooner—suddenly he had three. Captain Bex convinced himself that the maintenance for one could be geared up to tackle all three. Since then it has been a year-round job keeping the vessels in sailing shape. Assisted by his wife Ann, Captain Bex works to maintain all three schooners, hires their captains and crews, sees to advertising and publicity, and books the passengers. Until a short time ago, he also captained the *Mercantile* on her weekly cruises from June through September. During his years at the helm, he has seen many interesting things.

One day outside Bass Harbor, three whales came alongside the schooner. "The tops of their bodies were out of the water, stretching from the stern to the foremast as they traveled with us, blowing water in the air," Captain Bex told me. "Another time we saw hundreds of porpoise leaping from the water between the Graves and Mark Island."

No one can guarantee the sighting of whales or schools of porpoise. Sailing along the Maine coast is sailing with nature and her ever-changing moods and sights. The only promise is that there will be no phones, no business, no worries: only a comfortable relaxed vacation as you sail among the islands.

Schooner MISTRESS on Penobscot
Bay.

HARVEY GAMAGE

Tonnage	**94 gross tons**
Length on deck	**95 feet**
Beam	**23 feet 7 inches**
Draft (full keel)	**9 feet 7 inches**
Sail area	**4,200 square feet**
Passengers	**32**
Crew	**7**

The *Harvey Gamage* is a gaff-rigged fore-and-aft schooner built in the Harvey Gamage Shipyard in South Bristol, Maine, in 1973. The schooner was designed by McCurdy and Rhoades, using the same lofting as the *Bill of Rights*. The physical differences between the two vessels were made by Harvey Gamage himself as he built them, reflecting his own personality into the design. The schooner was the 261st vessel built by Harvey Gamage; therefore, her owner, Eben Whitcomb, and his partners decided to name the schooner after him.

Constructed of native oak, fir, and pine, the vessel is a blend of traditional shipbuilding methods with the comfort and safety of modern technology. She is equipped with six water-

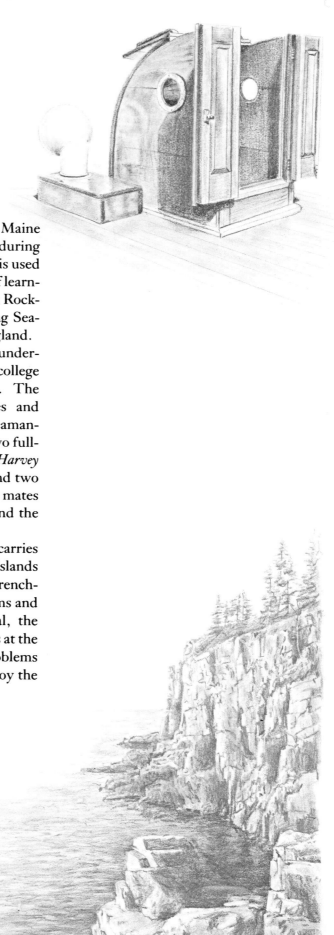

tight compartments and a 120 horsepower diesel engine.

The *Harvey Gamage* sails year-round, traveling in Maine waters in the summer and south in the Virgin Islands during the winter. On her spring and fall cruises, the schooner is used as a sailing college, taking students to sea for a semester of learning called a "Sea-Mester." The fall Sea-Mester begins in Rockland, Maine, and ends in the Bahamas, while the spring Sea-Mester begins in the Virgin Islands and ends in New England.

A sea-mester is a liberal arts program designed for undergraduate students. The student-sailors earn up to 16 college credits in a total maritime educational experience. The academic curriculum covers courses in the sciences and humanities—such as coastal ecology, navigation and seamanship, ichthyology, and literature of the sea, taught by two full-time faculty members as well as visiting lecturers. The *Harvey Gamage*'s ship staff includes the captain, three mates, and two cooks. The captain is the master of the vessel, while the mates are charged with the daily operation of the schooner and the instruction of the students in seamanship.

During her summers in Maine, the *Harvey Gamage* carries passengers on week-long cruises among the picturesque islands of Muscongus, Penobscot, Jericho, Blue Hill, and Frenchman's bays. Each week a lobster bake with steamed clams and corn-on-the-cob is prepared on shore. After the meal, the schooner's crew can often be found organizing crab races at the water's edge. It is a Walter Mitty world where the problems and hectic pace of everyday life are forgotten as you enjoy the romance of yesterday.

Schooner HARVEY GAMAGE
off Monroe Island.

ANGELIQUE

Tonnage	**99 gross tons**
Length on deck	**95 feet**
Beam	**23 feet 7½ inches**
Draft (full keel)	**11 feet**
Sail area	**5,129 square feet**
Passengers	**31**
Crew	**7**

The *Angelique* is a gaff-rigged ketch whose lines are similar to those of a Brixham trawler. She was designed by Imero Gobbato and Mike Anderson and built by Putnam Shipyard in Palatka, Florida in 1980. The *Angelique*'s hull is constructed of ⁵⁄₁₆-inch-thick steel plate. The vessel has twin screws powered by two 160- horsepower inboard diesel engines. Her masts are steel, but all other spars are made of Maine spruce. Although her hull was built in the south, most of her fittings and finish work have been done in Maine by local craftsmen.

The *Angelique*'s ketch rig is unique in the windjammer fleet. Unlike the schooners, her mainmast is forward and carries a much larger sail area than her aft, mizzenmast. Captain Anderson explained that this sail design reduces the size of each

sail, making it easier to handle, and has the distinct advantage of being reefed while underway. A schooner must be reefed before setting sail.

The *Angelique* is owned by Captain Mike Anderson, who helped design the vessel and did much of the construction. Captain Anderson knew what he wanted in a sailing craft as he worked on the *Angelique*. From the age of 14, when he sailed for six months with his family to Tahiti, he has been fascinated by the sea. For the past 15 years he has worked as everything from deck hand to captain on Maine waters. He captained both the *Mistress* and the *Mattie* prior to purchasing the *Stephen Taber* in 1974. Captain Anderson sailed the *Stephen Taber* for five years before building the *Angelique*.

"Each captain has a special pride in his vessel," he told me. "They are an extension of our lives."

Passenger comforts abound on the *Angelique*. She has private cabins with running water and full headroom. There are saltwater showers, a large centrally located dining room, and a spacious deckhouse that not only affords passengers a topside area for relaxing in any weather, but also houses the galley. Hearty meals are skillfully prepared by Captain Anderson's wife Myrna.

Distinguished by her ketch rig, plumb stem, fantail stern, and tanbark sails, the *Angelique* is a proud member of the windjammer fleet who is as much at home offshore as cruising among the coastal islands of Maine.

Ketch ANGELIQUE on Blue Hill
Bay.

HERITAGE

Tonnage	93 gross tons
Length on deck	93 feet
Beam	24 feet
Draft	8 feet
(centerboard down)	15 feet
Sail area	5,200 square feet
Passengers	35
Crew	6

The *Heritage* is a fore-and-aft schooner being built at the North End Shipyard in Rockland, Maine. Designed by Doug Lee with the assistance of several other master builders, the *Heritage* combines the strength of modern materials with the traditional methods of shipbuilding.

The lofting was completed and the keel laid in 1980, with a proposed launching in 1983. The *Heritage* is a joint partnership between Captains Doug and Linda Lee and Captain John Foss. Her designers feel the vessel's number one criteria is aesthetics—to look, act, and feel like an old vessel. However, her construction includes many modern features such as a steel band sheer strake embedded in epoxy resin to help keep her sheer from hogging or sagging out of line.

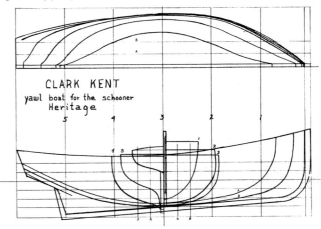

CLARK KENT
yawl boat for the schooner
Heritage

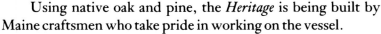

Using native oak and pine, the *Heritage* is being built by Maine craftsmen who take pride in working on the vessel.

Captains Lee and Foss, both master builders, look at the construction of the schooner as an evolution from the many old vessels they have restored.

"Putting the best of each into one, logical conclusion," as Captain Foss expressed it. An example is the increased dimensions of the lower strakes and their method of being fastened to the keel with ⅝-inch-diameter drift pins.

"The *Heritage* has been designed to last forever." Captain Lee told me.

The entire length of the keel has been fitted with a 12-inch by 12-inch mass of lead ballast, plus an additional seven tons of onboard ballast that will be used to adjust how the vessel sits in the water once she has been launched. Her forward deck house contains the schooner's power supply and a donkey engine. Below are three separate gathering areas with woodstoves for those cool summer evenings. Each cabin is equipped with running water and electricity. The galley and dining area are forward and captain's quarters aft.

The *Heritage* will move in and out of snug harbors pushed by a powerful yawl boat named the *Clark Kent*. Both the yawl boat and a sailing wherry named the *Lois Lane* have been built at the North End Shipyard and will be carried on the *Heritage*.

It will be an exciting day when the newest member of the windjammer fleet slides down the ways, continuing Maine's nautical heritage.

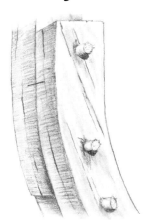

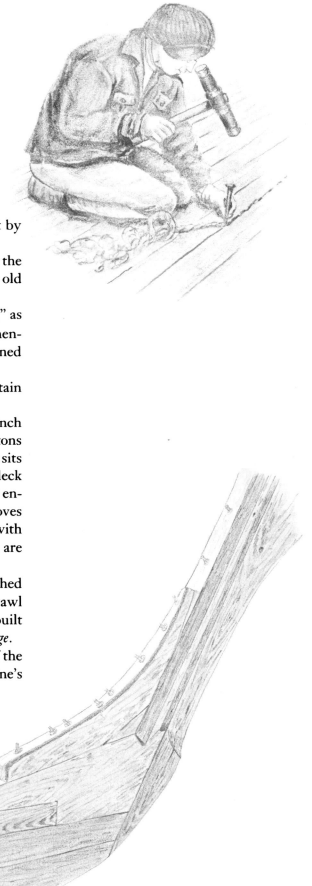

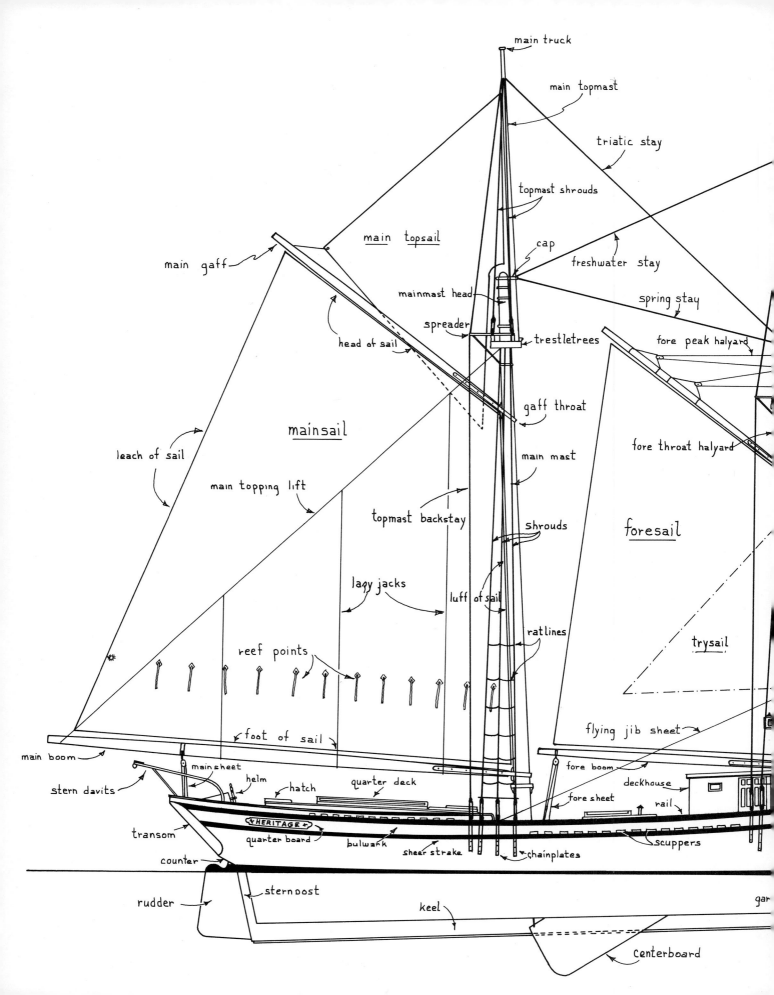

main truck

main topmast

triatic stay

topmast shrouds

main topsail

cap

freshwater stay

main gaff

spring stay

mainmast head

fore peak halyard

spreader

head of sail

trestletrees

gaff throat

mainsail

main mast

fore throat halyard

leach of sail

foresail

main topping lift

topmast backstay

shrouds

lazy jacks

luff of sail

trysail

ratlines

reef points

flying jib sheet

foot of sail

main boom

fore boom

mainsheet

helm

hatch

quarter deck

deckhouse

stern davits

fore sheet

rail

⋆HERITAGE⋆

scuppers

transom

quarter board

bulwark

sheer strake

chainplates

counter

rudder

sternpost

keel

gar

centerboard

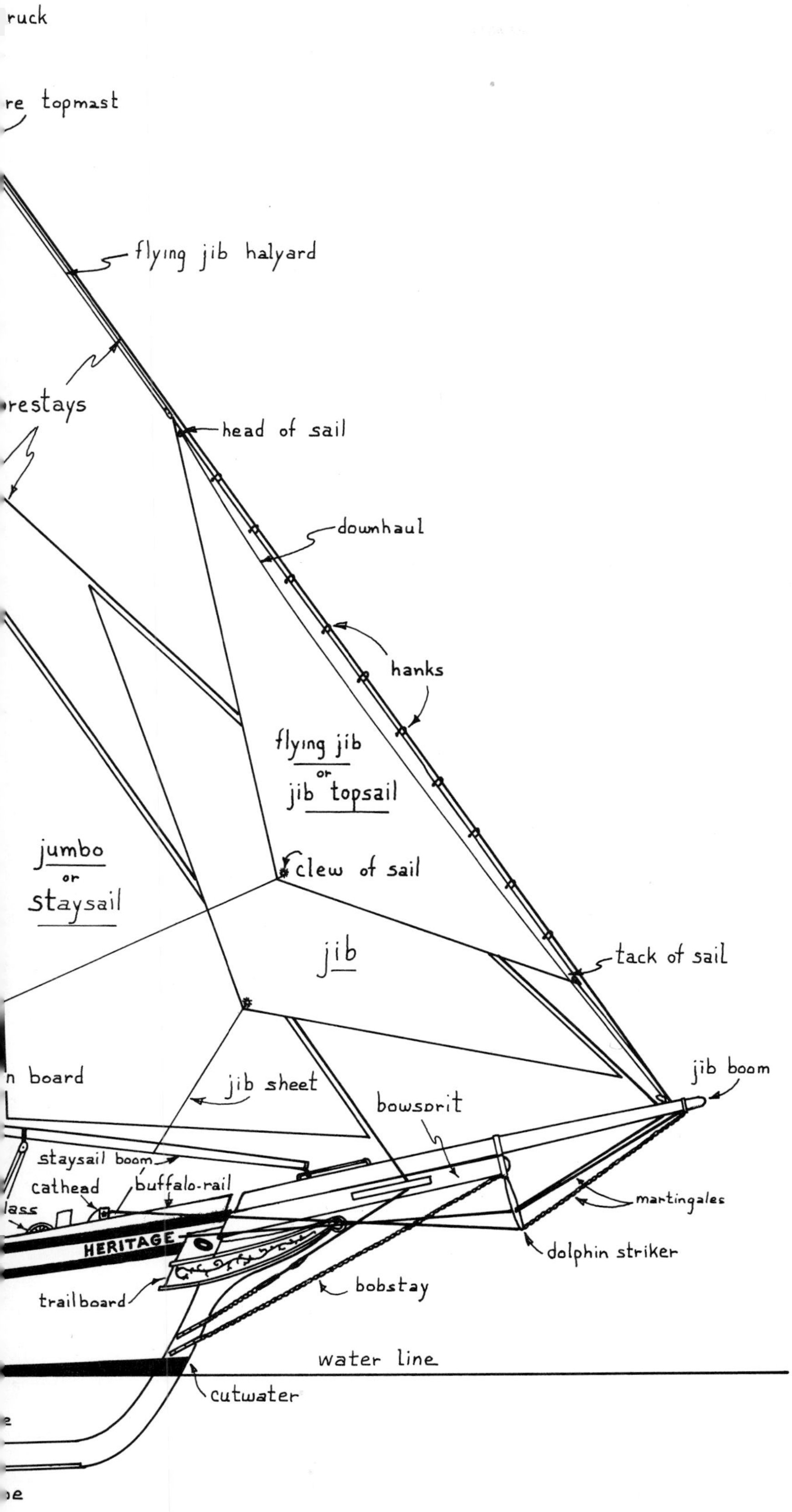

ruck

re topmast

flying jib halyard

restays

head of sail

downhaul

hanks

flying jib
or
jib topsail

jumbo
or
staysail

clew of sail

jib

tack of sail

jib boom

n board

jib sheet

bowsprit

staysail boom

cathead

buffalo-rail

martingales

lass

HERITAGE

dolphin striker

trailboard

bobstay

water line

cutwater

e

e

Schooner HERITAGE Sail Plan.
(Note: some details omitted
for clarity)

from my

Sketch

Book

great blue heron

eider

arctic tern

pollock

seaside lavender

puffin

kelp

ocean sunfish

flounder

sturgeon

moon jellyfish

tuna

cod

haddock

cormorant

blueberry

rock crab

rugosa rose

common tern

skate

hake

killdeer

barnacle

lady's slipper

seaside goldenrod

great black-backed gull

lambkill

seaside pea

harbor porpoise

mackrel

devil's paintbrush

Bonaparte's gull

lesser scaup

labrador tea

large blue flag

alewife

goldeneye

striped bass

Indian pipe

bald eagle

meadowsweet

seal

herring

lobster

bluefish

black chokeberry

osprey

halibut

rockweed ~ blue mussels

dolphin

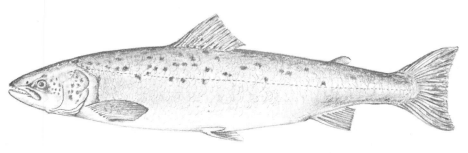

salmon

brown creeper

star flower

loon

black-eyed susan

chickadee

tall buttercup

110

Sunset over North Haven Island.

Addresses

ADVENTURE
Schooner ADVENTURE
Captain Jim Sharp
Box 696
Camden, Maine 04843
207-236-4449

ANGELIQUE
Captain Mike & Myrna Anderson
Yankee Packet Company
Box 736
Camden, Maine 04843
207-236-8873

SYLVINA W. BEAL
SYLVINA W. BEAL Cruises
Captain John Worth
Box 509
Belfast, Maine 04915
207-548-2922

NATHANIEL BOWDITCH
Schooner NATHANIEL BOWDITCH
Harborside, Maine 04642
207-326-4822

BOWDOIN
Schooner BOWDOIN
R.F.D. #1, Box 726
Rockland, Maine 04841
207-594-2301

VICTORY CHIMES
Schooner VICTORY CHIMES
Windjammer Wharf
Rockland, Maine 04841
207-596-6060 or 326-8856

MARY DAY
Coastal Cruises
Captain H. S. Hawkins
Box 798
Camden, Maine 04843
207-236-2750

ISAAC H. EVANS
Captain Douglas K. Lee
Box 482
Rockland, Maine 04841
207-594-8007

LEWIS R. FRENCH
Schooner LEWIS R. FRENCH
Box 482
Rockland, Maine 04841
207-594-8007

HARVEY GAMAGE
Dirigo Cruises
39 Waterside Lane
Clinton, Conn. 06413
203-669-7068

HERITAGE
  Schooner HERITAGE
  Box 482
  Rockland, Maine 04841
  207-594-8007

MATTIE
  Maine Windjammer Cruises
  Box 617
  Camden, Maine 04843
  207-236-2938

MERCANTILE
  Maine Windjammer Cruises
  Box 617
  Camden, Maine 04843
  207-236-2938

MISTRESS
  Maine Windjammer Cruises
  Box 617
  Camden, Maine 04843
  207-236-2938

J. & E. RIGGIN
  Captain Dave Allen
  Schooner J. & E. RIGGIN
  Box 571
  Rockland, Maine 04841
  207-594-2923

ROSEWAY
  Captain Orvil Young
  Schooner Roseway
  Box 696
  Camden, Maine 04843
  207-236-4449

STEPHEN TABER
  Captain Ken Barnes
  Schooner STEPHEN TABER
  70 Elm Street
  Camden, Maine 04843
  207-236-3520

TIMBERWIND
  Schooner TIMBERWIND
  Captain Bill Alexander
  Box 247-C
  Rockport, Maine 04856
  207-236-9063

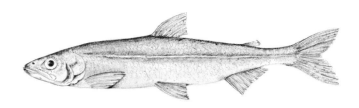

smelt

Glossary

A

ABAFT. Toward the stern; behind.

ABEAM. At right angles to the fore-and aft line in the center of the vessel.

ABOARD. Upon or in a vessel.

ABOUT. Around or rotation. The situation of a sailing vessel immediately after her course to the other tack.

ABOVE DECK. On deck.

ABREAST. Opposite or abeam of.

ACCOMODATION. Quarters on board.

AFOUL. Entangled, or collision of two ships.

AFT. At, near, or toward the stern.

AFTER. Farther aft; toward the stern.

AHEAD. Lying in the direction of a ship's course.

AIDS TO NAVIGATION. Buoys, beacons, fog signals, etc., placed in the interest of safe navigation.

ALEE. At or to the lee, or sheltered side; away from the wind.

ALEWIFE. A small, deep-bellied fish of the herring family.

ALGAE. Any of several different classes of marine plants, including kelp, sea lettuce.

ALOFT. Anywhere in the rigging or on the masts.

AMIDSHIPS. In or toward a ship's middle part.

ANCHORAGE. A place where a vessel is anchored or a suitable place to anchor.

ANSWER THE HELM. Respond to action of a rudder.

ASTERN. At any point behind the vessel.

ATHWART. Across; from side to side; at right angles to the fore-and-aft line.

AWASH. Level with, or emerging from, the water. Overflowed with water.

AWEATHER. At, to, or toward the weather side, or side from which the wind blows.

AWEIGH. Said of an anchor when its flukes are just clear of the bottom.

B

BACKSTAY. A rope or cable leading from the upper part of any mast to a ship's side abaft her lower rigging. Backstays serve as lateral support for topmasts to prevent them from swaying forward.

BACKWASH. A receding wave, or wash from a propeller turning in astern motion.

BAGGY WRINKLE. Type of chafing mat made by hitching many short manila rope-yards around two lengths of marline. The long, bushy product is wound around the rigging to reduce wear on a sail.

BAIL. To dip out water. Remove water from a boat's bilges.

BALLAST. Weight carried in a vessel for stability.

BALTIMORE CLIPPER. A fast vessel with a sharp "clipper" hull originating on the Chesapeake Bay and used as a privateer, characterized by an extreme aft rake in masts, deep sheer, and low freeboard.

BARE POLES, UNDER. Said of a sailing vessel when all sails are taken in.

BARNACLES. A general term for small crustaceans which fix themselves to ships' bottoms and other underwater structures.

BATTEN. Strip of wood or steel used for fastening or securing objects together. Also, splines of wood fitted in narrow pockets on some sails to keep the leach flat.

BEACH. To run or haul a vessel up on a beach. Land between high and low water limits.

BEAM. Extreme width of a ship. One of the athwartship structural units that support decks and stay the ship's sides.

BEAMY. Having a broad beam, usually greater than the average vessel length-breadth ratio, which is approximately 8 to 1.

BEAR. To be directed to any end or purpose. To alter ship's course.

BEARING. Direction in which an object is observed; direction of one object from another as indicated by a point of the compass.

BEAT. In sailing, to work to windward by alternate tacks.

BECALMED. Deprived of wind. Calm.

BEETLE. A heavy wooden mallet used in driving wedges, or in caulking.

BEFORE. Forward of.

BELAY. To make fast: to fasten a rope by winding it figure-eight fashion over a belaying pin or cleat.

BELL. Unit used on shipboard to announce each half hour of a watch. There are six watches of four hours each, with the first half hour of each watch being one bell.

BELOW. Underdeck.

BERTH. Bed or cot.

BIGHT. Loop or turn in a rope, as distinct from its ends.

BILGE. Part of a ship's hull extending outward from her keel to a point where her sides rise vertically. Lowest portion of a vessel inside her hull.

BINNACLE. A pedestal or case for housing a compass.

BITT. Strong, short post of wood or iron, usually fastened to the deck in pairs—used to secure lines and named according to their use.

BLOCK. A mechanical device for moving an object by means of a rope over its contained sheave. Blocks receive different names depending on their shape, purpose, and placement on board ship.

BOARD. To embark. To go on board.

BOBSTAY. Rope, chain, or bar from a bowsprit end to the stem for counteracting stress on the headstays.

BOLD. Deep, navigable waters very near to land.

BOLT-ROPE. A line sewn to the edges of a sail.

BONE IN HER TEETH. To throw up a foam or spray under the bow. Sailing fast.

BOOM. Spar used to spread a fore-and-aft sail, especially the foot of the sail.

BOW. Forward end of a vessel.

BOWLINE. A non-slip knot.

BOWSPRIT. Large boom or spar projecting forward from a sailing vessel's stem to meet stress on the fore-topmast stay.

BRACKISH. Salty and fresh water mixed.

BREACH. Breaking of water as waves or a surf. Also, leap of a whale out of water.

BREAKER. A small water cask. A wave breaking on a beach or rocks, etc.

BREAKWATER. A sea wall or deep-water pier for breaking the face of waves.

BRIG. Two-masted, square-rigged vessel with a fore-and-aft mainsail.

BRIGHTWORK. Unpainted woodwork on a vessel; also, polished metalwork.

BRINE. The ocean, salt water.

BRIXHAM TRAWLER. A sailing vessel, generally ketch-rigged, found chiefly in the North Sea, built in Brixham, England having a plumb stem, raked sternpost, and a counter stern.

BROACH. When running with a high sea, to be turned broadside by accident.

BULKHEAD. Upright partitions separating various compartments in a vessel.

BULWARK. Strake of planking forming an extension of the vessel's side above her deck.

BUMPER. A buffer or fender.

BUOY. A floating marker used in navigation.

BUTTOCK. That part of a vessel's stern above her waterline.

BY. Denoting near to or in position.

C

CABIN. A room on board ship.

CAULK. To drive oakum or cotton into seams of planking on a ship to prevent leakage.

CANT. To place in a position oblique to a definite line, inclined to one side.

CAPSTAN. A vertical drum revolving on a spindle used for heaving on a rope or anchor-cable.

CAR. A floating box for keeping fish, lobsters, etc.

CASK. A barrel-shaped wooden vessel for holding liquids.

CAT. A purchase by which an anchor is hoisted to the cathead.

116

CATHEAD. A piece of timber projecting from each bow at forecastle deck for hoisting anchor and for supporting it.

CAT'S PAW. Light air that temporarily ruffles the surface of the water.

CEILING. The planking fastened to inner surfaces of frames, forming the inner skin and adding strength in a vessel.

CENTERBOARD. A flat, movable, metal or wooden plate enclosed in a watertight housing used on shallow draft vessels to reduce leeway movement.

CHAIN LOCKER. Compartment for stowage of anchor chain.

CHAIN PLATE. One of the flat pieces of iron fastened vertically to the hull for securing lower deadeyes or ends of shrouds and backstays.

CHART. A map; a projection on paper of a portion of the ocean or other body of water showing land elevation, aids to navigation, depth of water, nature of bottom, and danger areas.

CHECK. To slack or ease a rope.

CHEEK. Projection on a lower mast which supports trestle-trees.

CHOCK. A block or wedge used to prevent a movable object from rolling or shifting. Also, a fair-lead for a hawser.

CHOPPY. Short, rough seas.

CLEW. The lower, aft end of a fore-and-aft sail.

CLUB. A small spar along the foot of a staysail or jumbo.

COASTER. A coasting vessel; a vessel that stays close to shore.

COLLAR. An eye or bight on upper end of a stay or shroud to fit over a masthead.

COMPANIONWAY. A stairway leading below deck.

COMPASS. An instrument used to aid in navigation which indicates direction on the earth's surface.

CORDAGE. Ropes, lines, wires, namely running rigging.

COURSE. Point of the compass to which a vessel is directed.

CRAFT. A vessel or boat; vessels of any kind.

CREST. Curling top of a wave.

CRINGLE. An iron or rope strop or grommet on bolt-rope of a sail.

CROSSTREES. Two pieces of wood or metal laid athwartship on the trestle-trees and forming a foundation for the top, or platform at lower masthead, also used for spreading and securing topmast shrouds.

CRUSTACEAN. One of a large class of hard-shelled animals including lobsters, crabs, shrimp, barnacles, etc.

CUDDY. A small room, cabin, or cupboard.

CULLING. Act of sorting fish, clams, crabs, etc. according to size and quality.

CUTWATER. Projecting timber bolted to fore side of a vessel's stem. Commonly used to denote the forward edge of the stem.

D

DAVIT. A curved or straight-armed crane for lifting and lowering boats, anchors, etc.

DAVY JONES. Spirit of the sea; the devil.

DEADEYE. A stout, flat and rounded block of hardwood, pierced with leading holes, through which a lanyard is reeved; fitted at the ends of shrouds, stays, etc.

DEVIATION. Error caused in a magnetic compass by a ship's own magnetism.

DINGHY. Any small, handy boat.

DISEMBARK. To put ashore from a vessel.

DITTY BAG. Small canvas bag used to hold twine, marline, sewing palm, needles, marline-spike, and other repair tools.

DOCUMENT. To register, or license a vessel as required by law.

DOLPHIN. A heavy mooring post either on a dock or in the water; the latter is secured to the bottom by a rope or chain fastened to an anchor. A marine mammal.

DOLPHIN STRIKER. A martingale boom suspended from the bowsprit. Also, dolphin boom.

DONKEY ENGINE. A small engine used on larger sailing vessels for heaving anchor, pumping water, hauling cargo, or setting sails.

DORY. A flat-bottomed boat having high flaring sides, and sloping stem and stern that taper to a point. Used by fisherman on the banks off New England, etc.

DOUSE. To suddenly release, haul down, or stow sails.

DOWN. In the direction of a sailing vessel's lee or lower side.

DOWN EAST. A purely American expression and refers to a region farther up the New England coast than where you are.

DOWNEASTER. A native of Maine.

DOWNHAUL. A single rope or tackle used to haul down a sail along the leech.

DRAGGER. A fishing vessel, smaller than a trawler, that makes its catch in nets dragged along the bottom.

DRAW. Term used to express how deep a vessel sits in the water; draft. *A ship draws nine feet.*

DRESS SHIP. Rig out a vessel with flags and pennants for display.

DRIFT. The distance a vessel moves to leeward, caused by sea currents and wind. Leeway.

DRIFT PIN. A steel pin or bolt used to align holes or hold members together.

DUE. Refers to direction; directly. *Due North.*

E

EARING. A short piece of rope used to secure a corner of a sail in position on a gaff or boom. Used for hauling out and securing a reef-cringle in reefing.

EASE. To lessen stress as on sheet or halyard.

EBB. Return or fall of the tide or a wave to seaward.

EDDY. Current of air or water running contrary to a main current.

ENSIGN. National flag or banner.

EYE. Loop or bight formed at a rope's end.

F

FAIR LEAD. A hole, roller, or sheave used to guide a rope in a desired direction.

FAKE. One of the loops in a coil of rope.

FAKE DOWN. To coil or lay line in fakes, either "figure eight fashion" or loops lying clear of each other to be free-running and avoid fouling.

FANTAIL STERN. The elliptical part of a hull projecting abaft of the sternpost.

FAST. Firmly fixed; held tightly.

FATHOM. Measure of depth equal to six feet.

FATHOMETER. Instrument for determining depth of water.

FEND OFF. To push or hold off, as in keeping a boat from striking a wharf or object.

FENDER. Anything acting as a buffer or cushion between two vessels' sides or between a vessel and a wharf, etc.

FETCH. To reach by sailing, as, *fetched the harbor.*

FID. A tapered wood or metal pin used to open the strands when splicing rope.

FIDDLE. A rack or small fencelike structure to keep dishes from sliding from a vessel's table; also, bars fitted across a galley stove to hold pots, etc. in place.

FIGUREHEAD. Decorative forward carving, usually in the form of a figure, immediately below a bowsprit and at the termination of the cutwater.

FIGURE EIGHT KNOT. Used as a stopper knot at a rope's end.

FISHERMAN'S STAYSAIL. A leg-of-mutton sail set between two masts.

FIX. Charted position of a vessel as determined by any number of methods; stars, soundings, radio, radar, etc.

FLEMISH COIL. A rope spirally coiled about its end.

FLUKE. The palm or flat part of an anchor which catches the ground.

FLUKEY. Uncertain or unsteady wind.

FLYING JIB. Loftiest and lightest jib.

FOLLOWING. Pursuing, as in following sea or wind.

FOOT. Lower edge of a sail.

FORE. A word used with other words to denote a part of the hull or rigging toward the forward end of the vessel, as foresail.

FORE–AND–AFT. From stem to stern. A fore-and-aft rig is one in which each sail is controlled by a single sheet and has the leech of the sail secured to a mast or stay. Schooners are of this rig.

FORECASTLE. That part of a vessel's weather deck forward of the foremast; also the crew's quarters in the forward part of the vessel. Sometimes fo'c's'le.

FORESTAY. Heaviest and lowest cable running from the stern to the lower masthead, which supports the foremast.

FORWARD. In, of, or pertaining to the forward part of the ship.

FOUL. Hindered or entangled; as fouled anchors; also not favorable, as foul weather.

FRAME. Any one of the skeleton members of a vessel's structure.

FREE. Loose, not secured.

FREEBOARD. Vertical distance from the top of the deck planking to the water.

FRESHEN. To increase in force, as a freshening breeze.

FULL. Said of a sail that is filled by the pressure of the wind.

FULL KEEL. A deep-draft vessel having no centerboard.

FURL. To roll up or gather a sail to its spars when not in use.

FURNITURE. All that is not a permanent fixture, such as sails, ropes, instruments, etc.

G

GAFF. Spar that spreads the head or upper edge of a fore-and-aft sail. Its outer end is the peak; its forward end is the throat.

GALLEY. Kitchen.

GANGPLANK. Portable platform forming a bridge between ship and pier.

GANGWAY. An opening in the rail or bulwarks for passage of persons or cargo.

GARBOARD. A vessel's bottom plank laid next to the keel, called the garboard strake.

GIMBALS. Mechanism for suspending an instrument which enables it to remain in constant plumb or level, unaffected by the ship's motion.

GONG BUOY. Buoy having two or more gongs of different tone that are struck by suspended hammers, activated by wave motion.

GRATING. A wooden cover of latticework laid over a hatchway to allow light and air to enter below.

GROG. An unsweetened drink of spirits and water, usually diluted Jamaican rum.

GROMMET. Ring or strop such as on an oar or yard; also, a metal eyelet sewn in a sail or piece of canvas.

GROUND TACKLE. Anchors, chains, windlass, or all gear used in conjunction with the anchor.

GUNWALE OR GUNNEL. Uppermost plank strake on the body of a vessel. Upper edge of a boat's side.

GYPSY. A drum with raised flanges projecting from a windlass, for the anchor chain to wrap around.

H

HALYARD. Rope by which a sail is hoisted or set. A gaff rig has both a peak and a throat halyard, which must be hoisted together.

HANDY. Said of a vessel that is easily managed or sailed.

HANK. A U-shaped metal fitting that secures the luff of a jib or staysail to its stay.

HARD. To full extent, as *Hard alee!*

HATCH. The coverings over openings in the deck.

HAWSEPIPE. The metal-lined opening in the ship's bow through which the anchor chain passes from the windlass to the anchor.

HAWSER. Any lengthy, heavy fiber rope.

HEAD. Foremost or projecting part; also a marine toilet.

HEADSTAY. General term that includes any of a vessel's foremast stays.

HEAVE. To draw, or haul as on a rope.

HEEL. To incline laterally or list. A vessel heels to some degree when sailing in heavy winds due to the force of the wind in the sails.

HELM. The wheel or tiller by which a vessel is steered. When a vessel responds to movement of the helm she is said to *answer the helm*.

HELMSMAN. Person who steers the vessel.

HIGHLINER. Fishing vessel that catches the greatest number of fish, is said to *have the high line*.

HOGGING. Bending of a beam or other structural part upward into a convex form. Rounding upward of a vessel's deck.

HOGSHEAD. Barrel-like receptacle; also, a measure equal to 63 U.S. gallons.

HOIST. To raise or lift, as hoist the sail.

HOLD. Entire cargo space below deck.

HOOP. A ring of bent wood that goes around the mast to secure the luff of a gaff sail to the mast.

HORSE. Any rope or bar on which a tackle-block slides.

HOUNDS. Projections at each side of masthead which support trestletrees.

HOUSE. Cabin or companion entrance; also, wheel house.

HUG. Keep close to shore.

HULL. Body of vessel.

I

IN STAYS. Also called "in irons." Heading into the wind with fore-and-aft sails luffing.

J

JACOB'S LADDER. Handy rope-sided ladder with wooden rungs used to go overside to get to and from yawl boat.

JAWS. The projecting parts of a gaff or boom that straddle the mast. Also called the throat.

JIB. Triangular-shaped sail set on a stay leading from a jib-boom or bowsprit to fore topmast head or above.

JIBE. To shift a fore-and-aft sail from one side of the vessel to the other when sailing before the wind; also, gybe.

JUMBO. A fore staysail set on the forestay, nearly right-angled in shape at its clew and provided with a boom along its foot.

JUMPER. Any preventer, as a rope which secures any object against being lifted out of position.

JURY. Makeshift.

K

KEEL. Main structural member, "backbone," of a vessel.

KEELSON. A structural member, similar to the keel, laid over the floors and bolted to the keel for added strength.

KEG. Small 10-gallon cask.

KELP. A type of algae or seaweed with stalks of great length and long, fringed, leathery leaves.

KETCH. Two-masted fore-and-aft rig having a larger mainmast forward and a smaller mast aft called a mizzen.

KITE. Any light, lofty sail.

KNEE. A crooked or L-shaped timber for stiffening and resisting stress.

KNOCKABOUT. Schooner sloop simplified in rig to the extent of dispensing with the bowsprit and setting a single headsail on the forestay.

KNOT. A unit of speed denoting nautical miles per hour, figured at 6,080 feet per mile rather than 5,280 feet per statute mile.

L

LANDLUBBER. One who lives on the land only; a sailor on his first voyage.

LANYARD. Piece of small rope for fastening or temporarily holding an object.

LAY. To place in position; to place one's self in a particular position.

LAZARET. A storeroom space; also, lazarette.

LAZY JACKS. A series of lines leading from one boom topping lift under the boom up to the opposite boom topping lift for keeping the sail from falling on deck when the sail is lowered.

LEAGUE. An old measure of distance equal to three nautical miles.

LEDGE. A ridge of rock near the shore; also, a shoal area at sea formed by rocks lying just below the surface or protruding slightly above the surface.

LEE. Sheltered side; that side protected from the wind or sea, opposite to weather side of vessel, opposite the windward side.

LEECH. The outer vertical edge of a sail.

LEEWARD. Toward the direction opposite the wind.

LEG-OF-MUTTON. A sail having a horizontal foot and a jib head.

LIFEBOAT. A boat equipped with supplies and

gear used to carry passengers and crew in the event of the necessity to abandon ship.

LIFE JACKET. A jacket made of buoyant material which is secured to the body to keep a person afloat.

LIGHTER. A vessel, usually without power, used for loading and unloading larger vessels lying in the harbor.

LIGHTHOUSE. A structure displaying a light of distinguishing characteristics such as color, angle, or sequence—used by mariners as a night time aid to navigation.

LISTING. Inclined or heeling to one side.

LIVELY. To move briskly or vigorously.

LOFTING. The layout of a ship's lines, full-size, on a flat surface. Measurements and patterns can be made from this drawing for all parts of the ship's structure.

LOG. Any of several types of devices used to measure a ship's speed. A record of a ship's speed, progress, etc.

LUBBER. An awkward or unskilled sailor.

LUFF. Forward edge of a sail; the action of a sail when the wind is passing over both sides at the same time.

L.W. Abbreviation for low water.

M

MAINMAST. Heaviest and second mast from forward in a fore-and-aft-rigged schooner.

MAINSAIL. Largest sail bent on the mainmast.

MAKE. To arrive at or sight a place, as to *make the harbor.*

MAKING–IRON. Tool used to caulk seams.

MANILA. The hemp or fiber of a species of banana tree used to make cordage.

MARE. Latin for the sea.

MARITIME. Situated or living near the sea.

MARLINE. To tie or bind: small stiff line.

MARLINESPIKE. A sharp spike-like instrument used in rope work.

MARTINGALE. One of two or more chains extending from lower side of a jib-boom to the lower end of dolphin-striker to distribute stress on the jib stays.

MAST. A spar or pole of wood or steel which supports a vessel's sails.

MASTER. Officer in command of a merchant or fishing vessel, also captain.

MASTHEAD. Upper part of mast between crosstrees and cap.

MATE. Officer next in command to the master.

MAYDAY. An international word used as a signal of distress.

MESS. Place or room on board in which meals are served; also, mess room.

MISS STAYS. Failure to come about when attempting to place a vessel on a new tack; in irons.

MIZZEN. After sail in a ketch or yawl; also, third mast or sail on a three-masted fore-and-aft schooner.

MOOR. To secure a vessel by means of anchors or hawsers.

MOUSE. A knot of yarn or Turk's head on a rope; also, a light line fastened across the mouth of a hook to prevent the hook from being disengaged.

MUDFLAT. Shoreland or tidal flats that are covered with salt water by the daily tides.

N

NAUTICAL MILE. 6,080 feet per mile as opposed to a statute mile, which is 5,280 feet.

NAVIGABLE. Having sufficient depth and width to allow passage of the vessel.

NEAP TIDE. A tide of minimum range occuring at the first and third quarters of the moon.

NECK. A narrow stretch of land.

NETTING OFF DORY. Fishing with nets from an open dory.

O

OFF THE WIND. When a vessel is sailing with the wind astern. A fair wind.

OILSKINS. Foul weather gear.

ON THE WIND. Sailing in a direction toward the wind. Beating.

OSPREY. Fish hawk; a large bird of prey which hovers high above the water until it spots a fish, then dives into the water to capture its prey.

OUTFIT. All equipment and supplies placed on board for a voyage.

OUTHAUL. A rope used for hauling out a sail on a spar.

P

PAINTER. Length of rope permanently secured to the bow of a boat.

PARREL. A rolling collar that holds the open part of the throat of a hoisting yard to its mast.

PAWL. A short piece of metal, pivoted on one end to allow it to drop into a toothed wheel on a windlass to stop the wheel from reversing.

PAY. To ease or allow to run out. *Pay out a line.*

PEAK. Outer end of a gaff.

PEAK HALYARD. The line by which the peak end of a gaff is raised.

PEEL. Broad part of an oar.

PILOT. Helmsman; person licensed to guide vessels along navigational routes into harbor.

PILOT HOUSE. Enclosed space or house on ship's bridge sheltering helmsman and equipment.

PILOT VESSEL. A vessel that carries pilots to and from waiting offshore vessels.

PLUMB STEM. The upright continuation of the keel at the bow perpendicular to the water line.

POINT. One of 32 divisions of the compass equal to 11¼ degrees.

POOP. Raised deck at after end of vessel. A ship is "pooped" when a large following sea comes over the stern and breaks on board.

PORT. Facing forward, left side of vessel, formerly called larboard. Any opening or door in a vessel's side for admitting air or light. Any harbor or area where a vessel can find shelter.

PRIVATEER. Privately owned vessel authorized to destroy or capture enemy vessels in exchange for all or part of the take.

PROW. The forward end of a vessel's hull above the water.

Q

QUARTER. After part of the side of a vessel.

QUARTER–BITTS. Posts at the after end of a ship for securing mooring lines.

QUARTER–BOARDS. Decorative extensions of the bulwarks often bearing the vessel's name.

QUEEN. A triangular sail set on the main-topmast stay.

R

RAFTED. Several vessels moored together, one on a mooring or anchor, the others tied alongside or to each other.

RAKE. Inclined from the perpendicular, as in the rake of the mast.

RATLINES. Ropes or boards fastened across a vessel's shrouds which form a ladderlike structure into the rigging.

REACH. A continuous, unbroken stretch of a river, or body of water with land masses on either side.

READY. To perform preparatory work for some other action.

REEF. To partially furl a sail to make the sail area smaller in high winds.

REEF KNOT. Square knot.

REEF POINT. A line fitted in a grommet used in reefing a sail; also, a ridge of rocks or sand, at or near the sea's surface.

REEVE. To pass the end of a rope, etc. through a block, dead-eye, or any opening.

RIG. Arrangement of masts, rigging, and sails.

RUDDER. The flat, vertical piece of wood or metal that is fitted at the after end of a vessel below the waterline, by which the vessel is steered.

RUNNING RIGGING. All movable lines on a sailing vessel used to control sails, booms, yards, etc.

S

SCREW. Propeller.

SCUPPER. An opening for carrying off water from a deck.

SCUTTLE. To sink.

SEINER. A large vessel used to carry a lengthy net for capturing fish that swim near the surface in schools.

SHEER. Upward curve of a vessel's upper lines from amidships toward both ends.

SHEER STRAKE. The heavier strake just below the bulwarks.

SHEET. A line running from the clew on the boom near the clew to the deck used to extend the sail to best use the wind.

SHOAL. Shallow.

SHROUD. Part of a vessel's standing rigging, which laterally supports the masts and bowsprit.

SOUND. To measure the depth of water, as with a lead-line. Also, a wide channel or inlet.

SPAR. A general term for any of the round members such as masts, booms, yards, etc.

SPLICE. Joining of two rope ends or parts by interweaving the strands.

SPREADER. A bar or spar used to spread one or more stays.

SPRING TIDE. A tide of maximum range occuring at the new and full moon.

SPRIT. A spar secured at an angle to the mast of a fore-and-aft rig which supports a quadrilateral sail at its peak.

SQUALL. A suddenly rising strong wind.

SQUARE–RIGGED. Having some principal sails of square shape and spread on yards.

STANCHION. An upright post used for supporting a deck, rail, or safety line.

STANDING RIGGING. All *fixed* ropes and cables which permanently support a sailing vessel's spars.

STARBOARD. Facing forward, the right side of a vessel.

STAY. Part of standing rigging to support masts in the fore and aft direction.

STAYSAIL. Triangular-shaped jib.

STERN. The extreme after end of a vessel.

STOPPER A short rope used to temporarily take the stress on a hawser or halyard.

STOW. To pack away.

STRAKE. One of the rows or strips of planking that make up the outside surfaces of the hull.

T

TACK. Lower forward corner of a sail; to come about, thus going from one tack to another by turning the vessel so the wind is brought to the other side of the sail.

TACKLE. A purchase, or set of blocks in which rope is passed to obtain a mechanical advantage.

TAFFRAIL. The ornamental rail around a vessel's poop or stern.

TANBARK SAIL. A dark, ruddy colored sail.

TEND. To stand by or watch.

THROAT. The upper forward corner of a gaff that fits around the mast.

TIDAL POOL. A saltwater pool left in a depression on the shore at low tide. The water is replenished at each high tide.

TIDE. The alternating rise and fall of the ocean's surface due to the joint action of the sun and moon, occuring every 12 hours and 25 minutes.

TILLER. An arm fitted to the rudder post for turning the rudder.

TOPMAST. Small mast extending above a lower mast which holds a small top sail.

TOPSAIL. Small sail set on a topmast above the gaff sail.

TRAIL BOARD. An ornamental plank on either side of the cutwater.

TRANSOM. The frame unit constituting the aftermost transverse structural member of the hull.

TRANSOM BOARDS. The stern of a boat.

TRESTLETREES. Pieces of wood fixed fore-and-aft on a mast at each side, forming a foundation for crosstrees.

TRIM. To adjust the sails as necessary to achieve the best use of the wind.

TUMBLE HOME. Inward curve of a vessel's sides above the waterline.

V

VEER. To pay out or allow to slacken.

W

WAKE. Track left in the water by a moving ship.

WEIGH. To raise a vessel's anchor from the sea bottom.

WHARF. A structure of wood, etc. at which vessels are berthed for unloading and loading.

WHERRY. A small, open pulling boat used for carrying passengers, usually rigged with a single mast and a loose footed sail.

WINDJAMMER. A sailing vessel, originally so

called by seamen on early steam vessels. In the late 1930s, a term used by Captain Frank Swift for his cruise schooners.

WINDLASS. A winch for heaving in an anchor cable, usually installed on the forecastle head.

WINDWARD. In the direction from which the wind is blowing, opposite of leeward.

WING AND WING. Sailing before the wind with mainsail set on one side of the vessel and the foresail on the other side.

Y

YARDS. A cross-spar for spreading the head of a square sail, etc.

YAWL BOAT. A small, powerful motor boat used to push or pull a fore-and-aft schooner in and out of harbors, often carried on stern davits while under sail; also, a fore-and-aft rigged boat with mainmast stepped forward and small mizzenmast stepped aft of the helm.

Z

ZEPHYR. A gentle breeze.

ZIG–ZAG. The forward path, turning at sharp angles from side to side, which a vessel must take to sail toward the direction of the wind.